Whatever It Takes

by Arlette Schweitzer

with assistance from
Paula Crain Grosinger, RN

God bless you

Arlette Schweitzer

WHATEVER IT TAKES

Author - Arlette Schweitzer
With writing assistance from Paula Crain Grosinger

Front cover photo by Roman Sapecki, Westerville, Ohio
Back cover photo - Schweitzer family photo
Publisher - Crain Grosinger Publishing, Mandan, North Dakota
Editor - Paula Crain Grosinger
Senior Editor - Brian D. Grosinger
Typesetter - Lynn C. Beck

International Standard Book Number: 09720054-2-0
Printed in the United States of America by
Sentinel Printing, St. Cloud, Minnesota

ACKNOWLEDGMENTS

*The publisher would like to thank the
following for their able assistance:*

Andrea Winkjer Collin, Smoky Water Press, Bismarck, ND

Donald Hoffman, Verda Publishing, Bismarck, ND

Peggy Reynolds, Photographer, Mandan, ND

Roman Sapecki, Photographer, Westerville, OH

*A special thanks from the author and publisher
to the wonderful
Sisters of the Presentation of the Blessed Virgin Mary,
Aberdeen, SD*

*I love my children, my family, Danny's family
and our friends – but this book is dedicated to the
love of my life, Danny Ray Schweitzer.*

*He has been my champion, supporting me in all that I do. Whether
it is an interview for television or a reading in church, he tells me
how terrific I am.*

*To him I am beautiful, witty and talented.
I know how blessed I am to have the generous
and glorious gift of his love and encouragement.*

Thank you, Danny. I love you.

*A special thank-you to my mother, Mary Friesz Rafferty.
You are the most selfless mother ever
and your seven children adore you.*

FOREWORD

I first learned of Arlette Schweitzer through media accounts describing her amazing role in the birth of her grandchildren. Like many, I read the headlines and admired the woman who was capable of such an undertaking on behalf of her daughter. It was a brave and selfless choice.

Arlette has an unshakable belief in family and in God. She also has a strong sense of purpose and is a survivor in the true pioneer spirit.

My partner and wife, Paula, met Arlette at an event in Rapid City, South Dakota, in 1992. Arlette gave Paula a copy of her manuscript to take home. Late one Saturday night, after I had already fallen asleep, Paula nudged me awake. She couldn't wait until morning to tell me she thought we should publish the story.

Publication of Arlette's book after a movie has already been produced may seem redundant. I assure you, it is not.

"Whatever It Takes" describes how one woman's vision and faith prompted her to become the first American, and only the second woman in the world, to bear her own grandchildren. Moreover, the book simply and elegantly conveys the message that ordinary people can do extraordinary things, even in the face of incredible obstacles. That is the same message we at Crain Grosinger Publishing try to convey with all of our projects.

-Brian D. Grosinger, Senior Editor
Crain Grosinger Publishing

The Rafferty House in Lemmon, South Dakota, where Arlette was born in 1948. Arlette's grandfather, John Rafferty, built the home.

Preface

As women, our lives are often distinguished by stages – childhood to young womanhood, to childbearing and childrearing, the onset of menopause, caregiver roles and even widowhood. While our male counterparts have their own transitions and share in our life experiences, their life stages are not as clearly demarcated by biology, nor as strictly defined by social norms.

Most of our gender experience the onset of menarche and the monthly reproductive cycle. For those of us who choose to bear children, there are again physical stages which men can only share vicariously.

Growing up in the 1950s and 1960s I saw remarkable changes in the expected roles of women. While women had previously been in the workplace, our opportunities were often limited. In the last half of the 20th century, we moved into career and leadership positions in ways that challenged societal norms and open doors like never before.

I am well aware of how fortunate we are. There are women in other places who have been forced to expect less, and to endure lives of desperation. It's wonderful that in this time, and in this country, most of us are afforded the opportunity to do the unexpected, to find solutions that go beyond conventional thinking. Sometimes those solutions even allow us to be fulfilled at the most conventional levels.

The events of 1991 are now medical history. I never intended to make history. Neither did I intend to challenge the medical establishment, religious norms or social order. My husband Danny and I had been blessed with a loving partnership. We were fortunate to have our lives enriched by both the joys and struggles of raising children.We simply wanted to allow our daughter and son-in-law to enjoy fully the privileges and responsibilities of parenthood. It was a gift that seemed so natural and so rational. I also believed it was within my power to give, though none of us imagined where the journey would take us.

Our lives have returned to the normal rhythm of ups and downs. The attention and public curiosity have thankfully subsided. While exciting and remarkable, the events of 1991 and 1992 were not the defining moments of my life, nor were they the most rewarding.

My belief that God provides the means, but we must take the action, has never faltered. We live in a time when medical science has produced new possibilities. Some of these alternatives are so radical that the ramifications haven't been considered – that is until someone comes along with a need or desire and asks, "What if?" So, this story is for all of you who dare to ask that question.

I believe we can accomplish miracles if only we are willing to do whatever it takes. I also believe there are many small miracles that occur every day of our lives. Sometimes we're too busy, too tired, or just too wrapped up in other events to appreciate these minor wonders.

I hope my story will help you take notice of some of the hidden strengths and courage you possess. My family and I have been richly blessed, and I believe God has miracles in store for anyone who has the faith and the courage to look for them.

Chapter 1

Heartbreak 1984

Late summer can be beautiful on the northern plains. The sky takes on a lovely aquamarine color punctuated by gentle clouds. The storms of June and July usually give way to solid sunshine. I especially savored those summer days just before the start of school.

It was one of those fine August days in Aberdeen, South Dakota. The windows and doors of our home were opened wide, filling the house with summer warmth and allowing me to enjoy the songbirds' chorus in the yard.

Our grandson, Lucas, was spending the day with me as he had every day that summer while I was off from my job as a school aide. While I rocked him to sleep, the phone rang causing him to stir gently against my chest. Most calls these days were for our teen-age daughter, Christa. I was sure I would disappoint the caller, because Christa was at the doctor for a checkup.

At age fifteen, Christa hadn't yet started to menstruate. Although I wasn't terribly concerned, I made an appointment for her with her pediatrician, Dr. Heinemann. I didn't accompany her to the appointment because neither of us thought it was a big deal. Besides, I was watching four-month-old Lucas. Christa had her permit to drive – so after picking up a friend she went to the clinic.

Balancing Baby Lucas on one hip, I reached for the phone and greeted the caller. I recognized Dr. Heinemann's voice and I immediately had a premonition this was going to be bad news. My stomach tightened into knots as Dr. Heinemann's words soaked in.

"I think you'd better come down here," Dr. Heinemann tried to sound reassuring. "I'm sending Christa to the hospital for an ultrasound and you'll want to be with her."

"What's the matter?" I asked, my voice sounding strange in my ears.

Dr. Heinemann said something about Christa's female organs – there was a chance she had only a partial uterus or maybe even no uterus.

The next few minutes were a blur. By fortunate coincidence my sister Marlis appeared at the screen door. I babbled something as I handed baby Luke to her. Then I dashed from the house.

I was opening the garage door just as my husband Danny pulled onto our driveway. He could tell from the distraught look on my face that something was terribly wrong. He hurried to my car and flung himself into the passenger seat.

"What's going on?" he asked as he closed the car door.

"Something is wrong with Christa and we have to get to the hospital right away," I explained disjointedly.

Danny, lacking the information that Dr. Heinemann had given me, jumped to the conclusion that Christa had been in some kind of accident – or worse yet that she was dying. When I explained what Dr. Heinemann had actually said, he was relieved. At least this wasn't a life or death emergency.

The twelve-block trip to our local hospital seemed agonizingly slow. Every stop sign, red light or slow-moving vehicle seemed like an obstacle. We wanted so desperately to get to Christa and support her during this upsetting time.

From the time Dr. Heinemann called until we arrived at the hospital, less then fifteen minutes had elapsed. Danny and I rushed into the hospital and headed straight to the x-ray department where we located Christa and her friend. They were sitting patiently and waiting for Christa to be called for her ultrasound. I sank into the chair next to Christa's.

"Mom, they don't think I have a uterus"" she said bravely.

Then the dam broke. I folded her into my arms and we both started to cry.

A little while later the ultrasound confirmed the grim prediction. Danny, Christa and I sat in a tiny room as Dr. Heinemann explained the situation to the three of us.

"You will need to go to the University of Minnesota for some more testing," she said. "Christa, you have what is called Mayer-Rokitansky-Kuster-Hauser Syndrome. Christa is missing her uterus and has a smaller

2

than normal vagina."

"After your checkup at the University, go home and put this on a shelf," she advised. "Don't think about it everyday. Don't worry about it until you have to worry about it."

We discussed details for the appointment at the University of Minnesota. It seemed like so much to absorb. Dr. Heinemann sensed how hard this news was on Christa.

"Christa, don't let this ruin your life," Dr. Heinemann tried to reassure her.

When we emerged from the hospital the day didn't seem so bright or sunny anymore. We felt numb and drained.

As a mother I wanted to make it "all better." Christa was my little girl and it was easy to make things better when a kiss on the hurt was all it took. But no kiss would heal this wound and I knew the ramifications would be deeper than the physical problem. Christa and I knew that with the diagnosis "no uterus" her lifelong dream was crushed. From the time she was very young, my daughter believed there was no more important job in the universe than to be a mother.

Later we were to learn Mayer-Rokitansky-Kuster-Hauser Syndrome involves varying degrees of abnormality and disability. Some girls are born with no vagina or a partial vagina, one kidney or horse-shoe shaped kidneys, one or no ovaries, spine and even bone malformations. The common denominator is that all of them are born without a uterus.

Dr. Heinemann had been wise to give us only the information we needed to know that day. She knew we would learn more at the University of Minnesota and wanted to give us time to absorb the initial diagnosis.

As we drove home, I knew the days ahead would be difficult for this child who dreamed of the day when she would have her own family. In my heart I also knew we had to trust that something good could come from this. I didn't know what that would be, but I had faith that God would provide us with answers.

"God has something special in store for you, Christa," I whispered to her. "I know He has."

The following days were a blur. I cried myself to sleep at night and I knew that despite her brave face Christa was suffering privately. Christa's dream to be a mother was no secret. As early as the first grade she had written in her school days book that she wanted to be a mommy. The same sentiment was added each year to that book.

Now in high school, Christa had just finished an essay on her life's vocation. A mature Christa reiterated her desire to be a mother and her belief that motherhood was a sacred and important calling. The essay was handed in during the school term before her diagnosis. When I later found it on her desk after her diagnosis, I wept. My heart ached as I read of her commitment to being the best mother she could be and what a grand vocation she felt motherhood was.

The very next week Danny, Christa and I were on our way to the the University of Minnesota for the dreaded appointment. On family trips Christa and I usually played cassette tapes, singing along enthusiastically, but on this journey we rode solemnly through the countryside. There were endless miles of silence.

In hopes of making this trip less serious and something of a mini-vacation, we made plans to meet Danny's brother, Mike, and sister-in-law Brenda in Minneapolis. We were going to incorporate some sight-seeing and a Juice Newton concert into our schedule. Perhaps we could distract ourselves from the grim purpose for the trip, if only for a little while.

As one of our parish priests had once said, "The road is bumpy and takes many turns. It may take you where you do not want to go. You are steering a two-seater bike, but the passenger in back is Jesus and He says, 'Keep pedaling.'"

The bicycle was slow but steady that day as we pedaled to Minneapolis.

Christa's appointment was early the next morning. The waiting room was below ground-level and the dreary office interior made me uneasy. When it was Christa's turn, Danny and I waited anxiously for the results. We were finally summoned to sit with Christa for a consultation with the doctor.

He shocked us by saying he felt Christa should have surgery to lengthen her vagina and he continued by telling us what the procedure involved. Skin would be harvested from her buttocks and thighs and then used to create a larger vaginal canal. We could hardly ask the questions we had formulated before we got there.

"What about Christa's ovaries, her kidneys, her hormone count, her bones?" we asked.

"Christa is a very lucky girl," the doctor patiently explained. "She has both kidneys and both ovaries. The good news is that everything is functioning perfectly. Her bones and hormone count are also fine."

Before we left, the doctor again stressed how fortunate Christa was. The relief Danny and I felt was only overshadowed by the prospect of the surgery the doctor had suggested. Christa was ready to go ahead with the surgery right then and there. If something was wrong, she wanted it made right, to be normal and to put this nightmare behind her. Danny and I needed a little more time to think. This was our little girl, our baby, and we had to make sure we made the right decisions. What we decided put us on the path of hope. What we didn't know is that the decision would thrust us into the limelight seven years later.

Chapter 2

Arlette Rafferty

The town of Lemmon is in north central South Dakota. If you stand on the railroad tracks you can put one foot in North Dakota and have the other foot in South Dakota.

This clean little burg of eighteen hundred people boasts an agate jewelry manufacturing plant where my father worked, and a petrified wood park that is one of the largest and best in the world.

My family takes a special pride in the park. It is part of our family legacy to the community. My grandfather, John Rafferty, was the contractor for the park when it was built during the Great Depression. My father and uncles all helped with locating and gathering the specimens of petrified wood as well as the actual construction of the park. I always felt the park was somehow our family property. Our house was just across the street and it seemed to be our personal playground. Of course, we happily shared with tourists and others in the community.

As a child, I felt the park was tangible proof that my family was important. We were poor, we did not own our home and we wore hand-me-down clothes, but look at the Petrified Park the Raffertys built! My grandfather's picture was even in the petrified museum in Lemmon, and I was so proud of the many stone and petrified wood things he made. These included headstones out of rock and petrified wood. As you travel South Dakota, especially the area near Lemmon, you see his markers in numerous cemeteries. His own grave, as well as that of my grandmother and my parents, are blessed with headstones made by Grandpa Rafferty's hands. When I visit those graves, I feel his love and presence. I know that this man played an important role in who I am, even though I never had the opportunity to meet him.

My earliest recollections are from when I was four years old. There were seven of us kids growing up in a two bedroom house. Our parents' bedroom was downstairs and my six older brothers and sisters and I slept in an upstairs bedroom that wasn't accessible from inside the house. We had to go outdoors, then up the stairs to our room. I recall a large bedroom with two double beds but I'm not certain if this is a real memory or simply what I've imagined from my siblings' accounts. Being the youngest of the brood I often listen to their stories about our Grandparents whom I never knew, and felt I had some acquaintance with things that happened before my time.

While I was still four, my family moved to another rented home where we lived for the next eight years. That is where most of my childhood memories took place. We called it the Demagall house because the owners were the Demagalls.

A tombstone in a cemetery near the North Dakota/South Dakota border. Made with petrified wood, this one was placed in the 1930s and may have been the work of John Rafferty.

Recalling the years at the Demagall house brings a flood of warm and happy memories. There were adventures and I especially enjoyed playing outside with my sister until dark.

We wouldn't come in until we heard the tune of our mother calling, "ARLETTE AND DARLENE, IT'S TIME TO COME IN!" Of course, that would be "the umpteenth time" as she would say.

Our neighbors across the street were the Nelsons and we spent many marvelous days and nights playing with them. They had even more children in the family than we did. Eleven I guess. Mr. Nelson was the town blacksmith, (yes, in the fifties we still had a blacksmith in Lemmon, South Dakota) and their huge yard was a trove of incredible stuff!

The Nelsons had a swing set minus the swings. This became our staging area for trapeze acts and other daring and dangerous contortions. There were intriguing machines. You could put a piece of tin in one and it would crank out a crinkled piece of metal which we later learned was corrugated. There was an old, paint-deprived building that once was a cook house. We christened it the "Yellow Store" and used the structure for games like *Ante I Over*. The interior of this building could become a store, a school, or our playhouse, depending on our flights of imagination. Often, our pretending extended into the night when this magical place would become the perfect stage for ghost stories and fortune telling with real candles.

The yard also boasted a well with a working pump. This was a glorious addition and perfect for those hot summer days when one of our favorite things was a water fight. Nowadays the Nelson's yard would be considered an accident waiting to happen, but with wondrous junk everywhere we thought it was heaven. There were enough stimuli to fill our imaginations through the long and wonderful summers of our youth.

We never lacked for things to do. Although money was something our parents worried about and didn't have enough of, the world of junk was treasure in our imaginations. We had something priceless that money couldn't buy.

It is said that smell evokes the strongest memories and I often experience this phenomenon. A whiff of gasoline transports me back to the corner gas station in Lemmon. It was run by our uncle Joe and looked like it was right out of a Norman Rockwell painting. I can see the local men sitting around chewing the fat, and I can hear the "ping" that announced a car had pulled up to the pump. This was back when there was real service. Everyone got their gas pumped and their windows washed from the comfort of their car. If Darlene and I had a few extra cents we'd run over to the station to buy five-penny sodas. Uncle Joe would always greet us as if he was surprised to see us saying, "Well, if it isn't Arlene and Darlette (his nicknames for us)."

The smell of menthol also brings back the delightful memory of my mother's treatment for a cold. When anyone in the family had a cold, we all got to sit on the "hot seat." There was a huge heat register that measured about four square feet in our kitchen. My mother would have us sit over it and cover us with a large blanket. Then she would put Vick's VapoRub in an earthen pot with a bit of water and place it over the heat register. As this combination heated up on the grate, the fumes would permeate our noses and lungs right down to our toes. The presumption was that if you were the one with the cold, these fumes would heal or burn the cold right out of you. If you did not have a cold, the treatment would stop the cold virus from entering your body. Or maybe it was Mom's way to get the entire brood to sit quietly for a while.

This memory is especially sweet because Mom would take turns holding us young ones on her lap. Mom usually didn't have the time to just sit and hold us, so this memory is one that I especially cherish. My memories also include sitting behind my father on the sofa and mussing his hair and then combing it, and curling up on my mother's lap while she cleaned my ears with a bobby pin. This was as close to physical expressions of love as my parents could give but we never doubted their love for us.

Winters on the plains are noted for being harsh. We still loved to do things outdoors when the weather permitted, but we had a whole list of things with which to occupy ourselves during those long cold snaps. Our indoor entertainment included endless games of cards, word games, and thinking games. Everyone in the family played and there were no special privileges because you were the youngest. You played and lost until you were wise enough to legitimately win. That was fine, and there was no trauma or disgrace in losing because the emphasis was on the fun of playing.

We also put together jigsaw puzzles. They were huge puzzles that the whole family did at the kitchen table. At meal times these puzzle masterpieces were covered with an oil cloth so we could eat without disturbing our work. All these thinking and problem-solving activities developed sharp minds and the ability to find creative solutions. I look back on those years and realize how important they were in making me the person I am.

Unfortunately, not all my memories are the warm fuzzy kind. In some ways we had a dysfunctional family, but that term was not popular then. We didn't know we were dysfunctional. We tended to think we had problems like everyone else.

Our dad Owen was an intelligent, witty Irishman with a drinking problem. He never missed a day of work as a lapidist at the agate jewelry manufacturing plant. But two evenings a week, Tuesday and Saturday nights he drank himself into a stupor. Tuesday was payday and Saturday was... well it was Saturday. On those two nights it was best to be out of Dad's way. The happy-go-lucky Irishman metamorphosed into a mean-mouthed, vicious and sometimes violent stranger. The only thing that saved us from coming to physical harm at his hands was the fact that my father was unable to come after us. Like many unfortunate people of his generation my father had been a victim of polio. The resulting nerve damage coupled with a disabling accident severely limited his mobility.

For as long as I could remember, Dad needed crutches to get around. Thus, after a few drinks of Everclear he couldn't maneuver the crutches well enough to do us much harm. The trick was to stay out of crutch reach and let the verbal barbs go in one ear and out the other. I mastered this concept but my sister Darlene enjoyed adding fuel to the fire. Sometimes she antagonized and baited Dad right out of his spot on the sofa. When this happened, all hell broke loose. Once, in a state of drunken madness, he tried to beat the bathroom door down, and with intoxicated strength he nearly did so. On the other side of that door, Darlene was trapped. Mom and I were frightened enough that we went outdoors and removed the screen allowing Darlene to escape out the window until things cooled off.

There were numerous times when Dad would go on a tear and Darlene or Mom would try to phone my married brothers for assistance. I often wondered what the telephone repairman thought. He became well acquainted with our house on the numerous occasions he was called to hook up our phone after my father had ripped the cord from the wall. After a night of yelling and threats, with ashtrays thrown at the television and crutch-swinging, we would go about our business the next day as if nothing had happened. We'd go to school or go about our usual activities, and in a way nothing unusual (for us) had happened. That was our life, that was normal, that was just the way Tuesdays and Saturdays were.

My mother, Mary Friesz Rafferty, was a tough, stoic German woman. She endured the hardship of never having enough money to feed and clothe seven children, let alone buy extras. She endured the tremendous burden of doing chores normally shared by husbands and wives. In those days the wives did the "women's work" and the men did things like fix the furnace, carry coal and ashes, put up the storm windows, etc.

Because of my father's disability, my mother not only washed, ironed, mended, cooked, and cleaned for this crew of nine, she also took on all the other chores. This was before automatic washers, dryers or heat that could be adjusted by a thermostat. She worked from four or five in the morning till late at night when she would quietly mend our clothes and stoke the furnace before retiring. We may have been poor but our house, our clothes and we children were scrubbed squeaky clean. There were many things Mother did not have the power to change, but her home and her charges were spotless.

I knew then that Mother suffered a great deal. She suffered physical exhaustion. She suffered from worry and sadness because she couldn't provide her children with the things other children had. She also suffered humiliation from relatives who not only had more, but who sometimes witnessed the "secret" that very few in Lemmon knew – that the Rafferty household had an eruption as dependable as Old Faithful two nights out of every week.

Today, schools and social services would intervene. Social workers would be watching and we would be every counselors' and psychologists' classic subjects. But in those days you pulled yourselves up and moved forward. You did what you had to do to survive. From this I developed my life philosophy: *DO WHATEVER IT TAKES*. With limited exceptions, I'm not sympathetic to those who blame the poor choices they make as adults on an unfortunate childhood.

I suppose because our family life was chaotic, most of my brothers and sisters left home at an early age. Clifford, the oldest, rode the rails with friends to go "out west" for work and schooling. He made his first trip when he was just fifteen years old and returned with amazing stories about his adventures. I will never forget the beautiful doll he and Mom bought for Darlene and me to share one Christmas. He was also a lifeguard at the local pool and made sure the rest of us kids had swim passes for the season.

Charles was our storyteller, specializing in chilling tales that kept the whole family on the edge of our seats. He celebrated his seventeenth birthday fighting in the Korean Conflict. Larry, the tough one, was our protector and made sure no bullies ever bothered us. He also joined the army when he was only seventeen. Both Larry and Charles made careers out of military life. My oldest sister Marlis married at sixteen.

After the first four of my siblings left home Jack, Darlene and I were left. There were intermittent furloughs and visits from our older siblings, but they had started to build their own lives. As a result, Jack had to fill many roles.

There was "Caretaker Jack," who had to drag Darlene and I along when he went to the movies. (He always made sure we sat well behind him.) There was "Jack the Parent," who walked me to school on my first day of kindergarten. He slowed down long enough to point at the building and tell me he'd be back later to retrieve me. He had another block to walk to his school, so in I went. There was "Baby-sitter Jack," who watched Darlene and me on Saturday mornings, allowing Mom her one and only outing of the week – a trip to the grocery store. There was plenty of belt-snapping and chasing on those mornings, although Darlene and I recall that we never did anything to antagonize Jack. By the time Mom was coming up the walk, groceries in hand, Jack had assumed his most innocent expression. We two little tattletales couldn't wait to give her a full report, but she would equitably turn a deaf ear to all three of us. It was the same every week.

Jack eventually joined the Air Force, leaving Darlene and me to find our own way. As each of our siblings moved on with their lives, it left a void and I missed them terribly.

My sister, Darlene, shares the brightest memories of my childhood. As an adult, she is one of my closest friends. Other than the two-year difference in our ages, we are very much alike and can spend hours on the phone.

As children, Darlene and I did everything together. Darlene read to me nearly everyday and through this activity I learned to read before I went to kindergarten. We owned only one real book but we went to the city library often. We would pick up books for our Dad who was an avid reader, and then we could take our time among the stacks carefully making our own selections. It was pure indulgence.

The one book that actually belonged to us was read over and over. It was *Uncle Arthur's Bedtime Stories*. Mom purchased the volume from a traveling salesman. It was one of the few luxuries she permitted herself to buy. At the time she had little notion of how influential that book would be. The stories dealt with honesty, values and moral character. A central theme of the stories was also the daily influence of Christ in our lives.

This book had a tremendous impact on my life and how I wanted to live it. I still have that cherished childhood copy and it has been shared with two more generations including my children and grandchildren. Because we only had that one special book, I think I learned to appreciate the value and importance of books.

Other than that marvelous red-covered book, we read mostly comics. I don't know that children today place the importance that we did on comics. It was absolutely vital that we get new comics every few weeks. Not having a lot of money to spend, we became quite enterprising in maintaining our comic supply. We developed our own trade network and scheduled Saturday morning trade events.

There would be a knock on the back door and we would find Buster Byers or another of the neighborhood boys with their boxes of comics. We would drag out our box, and then for the next couple of hours we negotiated transactions. One *Richie Rich* for one *Little Lulu*. One *Lil' Dot* and one *Baby Huey* for a thick *Archie*, and so on. This was serious business and without a doubt one of the greatest memories of my childhood. After each trading session, Darlene and I would take our new treasures up to our bedroom and spend the rest of the morning feasting on this wealth of reading material. We looked forward to Saturday trade days almost as much as holidays!

Darlene was my friend, my playmate, my teacher, and also my boss. She was the dominant older sister, yet she was also Mom's baby. I was the youngest in the family, but she was the baby of the family. She bawled when Mom hung out clothes in the winter. Mom made her cocoa every night for a bedtime treat, while she sat singing, "Give me my c-o-c-o-a."

This cocoa business bugged me so much that I decided I didn't ever want any cocoa. To top it all off, Darlene would come to bed with cocoa breath! She was a skinny kid and I think Mom worried that she was too frail. Mom should have just asked me because that skinny kid could get the best of me in a physical fight unless I could pin her down and sit on her with a pillow over her face. How this skinny Mama's baby got to be so bossy is an interesting question. If we played school she always got to be the teacher. Later when I became a real certified teacher I sent her a telegram with just four words: NOW I'M THE TEACHER!

I guess I was old beyond my years. Sometimes I think I was born old. Anyway, I wasn't young like my friends who had to ask permission to do everything. Darlene and I did what we wanted to do, within reason. In the summer we had to be home for meals and bed – but in between we were pretty much free. Sometimes we would get up at four in the morning and go lie on our garage roof until sunrise. I can remember the vast expanse of sky over the darkened plains. Lemmon didn't have enough city lights to obscure our vision of the stars and it was as if the heavens were wide open.

We would watch the sky until a faint glow started to color the eastern horizon. When the sun would start to appear, we would go throw pebbles at the Nelson girls' window to wake our friends, Helen and Betty, for an early start on the day. There was so much playing to do and we never wanted to waste a moment of the summer.

All week we ran and hiked and kicked up our heels but come Sunday, Darlene and I went to church. Sunday church was not unusual for most people. What was unusual was that just Darlene and I went to church. I'm not certain how or whose idea it was, but every Sunday the two of us would walk to church on our own. Not our church, or even a specific church, but any church! We might honor the Church of God with our presence for a few weeks then move on to the Presbyterians. One Sunday we even took part in a baptism by submersion in a cow trough at the Baptist church.

Darlene was seven and I was five when we started doing this. I can close my eyes and see the two little girls that we were, walking hand-in-hand to the church of our choice. I remember some of the sermons as well as many of the Sunday School lessons. Yes, we even went to Sunday School. The members of the various churches welcomed us, and if they thought this situation was strange they never mentioned it to us. Darlene and I were sad when ministers we liked moved on, yet we never actually discussed this rather odd arrangement. It just seemed the thing to do. To this day I have a profound respect for all denominations. I feel a kinship with many churches, and when I attend a wedding or funeral in another church I still feel comfortable.

Technology started to invade our world when I was about eight years old. First, the Nelsons got a television set. We were briefly awed by the transmitted pictures. Shortly after, we got a television. Helen and Betty sometimes had to be pulled away from their set to play. We also thought television was pretty great, but were really much too busy with our own adventures to pay it much attention.

News shows and sports were avidly watched by Dad. When the National Anthem was played, we were expected to stand with our hands over our hearts. Patriotism was instilled in all of us at an early age, and I still get tears of pride at the sight of a color guard bearing the flag or at the sound of the national anthem.

All four of my brothers served in the armed forces at one time or another, and I know my dad was proud of their service. I think my father would have liked to have served his country too, but his polio prevented that. It may have been one of the reasons for his bitterness when he drank.

During World War II our father served in the only capacity he could. He took my mother and their four children to Oregon by train, and like many others he worked in the shipyards. When the war ended they came back to Lemmon again by train. My mother wanted to stay in Oregon where many of her sisters and her mother had settled, but my father wanted to come back to South Dakota.

Mom recalled that trip home from Oregon as a horrible experience. She was left trying to control and entertain four youngsters while my dad spent the entire time in the smoking car playing cards. They arrived in Lemmon in the middle of the night. A snow storm was raging, but my Grandfather Rafferty was there with blankets and he bundled the kids up. Then he carried them one by one to the "petrified house" near the tracks that my parents would share with my grandparents. A few years later that is where I was born.

Mother dearly loved her in-laws. I never heard a disparaging word about them, and she spoke of them with only love and respect. This made an impact on me. My mom was my role model in life so I tried to be a good daughter-in-law and eventually a good mother-in-law.

My mother's mother was a kind German woman with many children. Marie Stelter married Christ Friesz when she was a young girl. She had a daughter out of wedlock when she met my Grandfather. Grandpa Friesz owned a large farm on the Cannonball River in North Dakota. He already had several children and had lost his first wife in childbirth.

The union of Marie and Christ produced my mother and several more children, but it was a hard life. This wasn't due to money problems but to Christ's stern, miserly and mean disposition. Mother's stories of her childhood included things like sledding and sleigh rides, swimming in the creek, exploring and finding rattlesnake dens, and Grandpa Friesz's bad temper. She talked about Grandpa chasing her around the farmyard with a pitchfork because she ran the tractor into a hole while making hay. She had to run to the neighbors' farm several miles away and take refuge with them until Grandpa cooled off.

Mom and the rest of her siblings left home as early as possible. She

The Rafferty family all together in the 1950s.

Back Row: Larry, Dad (Owen), Cliff, Mom (Mary), and Charles.

Front Row: Jack, Marlis, Arlette and Darlene

was just eighteen when she married my dad, hoping to find a better life.

In our family it was expected that if you wanted extras you would earn the money to buy them. All of us kids earned money in different ways. I got my first babysitting job when I was nine years old. Darlene and I baby-sat the children of our older brothers, our teachers and neighbors. We also sat the children of the man who delivered our coal. The money we earned was deducted from our parents' coal bill. It seemed like a fair and natural way that we could contribute to our family. Neither Darlene or I ever complained about this. I don't even remember this being part of any discussion. This was something we could do and we did it, never thinking we were making some big sacrifice.

Many of our babysitting jobs included cleaning and laundry. I actually enjoyed the cleaning, especially if there was a big mess. There is something satisfying about creating order from chaos and the results are usually immediate. I'll admit that this character trait has made me the object of some good-natured teasing and I'm sure a psychiatrist wouldn't have to do an in-depth analysis to determine what had influenced it.

Looking back, I think I gathered all the lessons of my formative years like one would gather eggs in a basket at Easter: patriotism, faith, Irish humor, German determination, a sense of right and fairness, hard work, a love of learning, the fun of playing, the challenge of winning and the joy of living. All my life has been a gathering and fortunately my basket always has room to add new experiences. Life, death, love, happiness, disappointment and heartache have all helped me grow. They all gave me the determination and strength I needed and would need.

It's as if family, friends, health and faith are the most important things in my basket. Those are the brightly colored Easter eggs. Then there are the things like my job, house, and car. Those are smaller chocolate eggs.

The basket can seem like it's full, but there is always room for some of those little jelly beans. The jelly beans represent all the small things that are nice to have, but that I could survive without. I try to keep my priorities straight and take care of the Easter eggs first. Then there is room for everything else. If I filled my basket full with jelly beans first, I'd have a hard time making room for the most important things.

Chapter 3

Danny

The single most important event of my life is when I met Danny Schweitzer. Danny's family moved to Lemmon when I was a mere fourteen. His father, Albert, was transferred to Lemmon to be the depot agent for the railroad. Danny was a handsome seventeen-year-old who had already graduated from high school.

Danny worked that first summer at the lumber yard and his sleeveless shirts, tanned arms and bulging muscles made my heart beat faster every time I caught a glimpse of him. But if the truth be told, I fell in love with his picture first. One of Danny's coworkers at the lumber yard was a mutual friend. When his wife showed me a photo of Danny, I fell back on the sofa in a theatrical swoon and declared to all around, "I'm in love, and someday I'm going to marry this man!"

Several days later, I was at this same friend's house scrubbing their floor. In walked Danny Schweitzer in person. I remember turning from my work and we looked at one another and there was this spark of connection. The chemistry was there and it was right.

We both had other steadies (a term used in the sixties). So we bided our time with flirting and friendship, even double dating with our steadies. When the four of us went to a movie, Danny and I always sat between the other two. Danny also was the driver and took his girlfriend home first. Both of us knew we had a strong attraction to one another but we cared about the people we were dating. Their feelings were important to us and we dreaded hurting them.

Danny's workplace was just across the street from my house, so he would saunter over on his break and after work. Soon we knew it was time to break from the old and start dating each other.

Danny and I talked for hours and discovered we shared many of the same feelings. We both loved animals, cared about people's feelings, and we both loved to laugh. This was a time when some guys would refer to their parents as "my old man" or "my old lady." I admired Danny because he always spoke about his parents with such respect and never fell into that bad habit. Although we shared so much, we came from dissimilar backgrounds. Danny's family structure was sound. They did not have money problems; he actually had a curfew, and his family went to church as a family. Because of these things, I felt inferior.

I lacked confidence anyway because the girls in my grade lived in stricter family environments. So, I hung around the kids in my sister's group. It was as if I had two lives. The schoolgirl Arlette had girl friends her own age, but at night and in the summer I ran with an older crowd. Thus, many of the people in my grade thought I was wild!

Cruising Main Street, going to the movies or to a Saturday night dance was about all there was to do in Lemmon in 1963. Groups of kids gathered to socialize and the worst thing we did was have a few beers. I personally did not drink, because I hated the taste of beer (and still do) but I stayed out late and had fun like everyone else in the older crowd. But wild I was not.

While I don't claim to have been wild, I didn't say I wasn't foolish. The next summer I was devastated but not shocked when I realized that this dumb fifteen-year-old was expecting a baby.

Danny and I cared a lot for each other... but marriage? I wasn't ready and I didn't think Danny was either. In the fall I would just be a high school sophomore. With the news of my pregnancy, my life literally turned upside down. When I told Danny of our dilemma, he immediately said we would get married. But I didn't want a marriage where the man felt trapped or coerced.

The day soon arrived when we had to tell our parents. The wheels were put in motion with little discussion and wedding plans were hastily made. I had confided to my oldest brother Clifford and his wife, Zada, about my predicament. They tried to be supportive, but this was not a happy time. I worried about my education, my friends, what people would say, and especially about my brothers, Larry and Jack. They were away at National Guard camp and would arrive home in time for the reception! My brothers were always protective of us girls and I wasn't sure if they'd come home wanting to kill Danny, or worse. Charles was overseas at the time so at least I didn't have to worry about brother number four for a while.

Danny and I took marriage instructions in his church, which was Catholic. As part of the instructions, I was required to sign a paper saying we'd raise any children we had in the Catholic faith. That was fine with me. My father was raised Catholic and although he did not attend church he still considered himself a Catholic. Strangely, in all of our church visits Darlene and I never attended our local Catholic Church. Only once had I even been in Saint Mary's, and that was only when our cousin, Diane, took us in to show us around. I remember going to the altar and kneeling but for some reason Darlene and I never went back again. Maybe we were in awe of the priest and nuns because of their garb. So, my second visit ever to a Catholic church was on my wedding day!

Danny and I were married August 22, 1964. Our wedding was a small affair. I was nearly numb allowing everyone who wanted to, to make decisions. In those days, there was very little pomp when a bride was already with child. I didn't even pick my own dress but let another sister-in-law bring one over for me to wear. Later, I wished I'd worn an attractive blue dress that I'd just worn once to sing at a school function. I don't even know where the cake came from, but I do remember that Cliff went to the bakery at the last minute to get a cake top. I remember him saying, "Arlette's got to at least have a top on that cake." I still have that keepsake of two bells of pink and white. When I look at it, I remember Clifford's kind and sensitive words from that day.

Danny's sister Kay was my bridesmaid, and her husband, Darrell Gill, was Danny's best man. In the Catholic Church in 1964, witnesses had to be Catholic. I think it was only the second time I had met Kay, and it seemed awkward and embarrassing to have her as my bridesmaid. My choice would have been Darlene had she been Catholic, but that could not be. Today, Kay and I are as close as sisters and I love her dearly, but on my wedding day she was a stranger.

My parents had mentioned the wedding to no one outside of our immediate family. Danny's family included his parents, his five-year-old brother, Mike, Kay and Darrell, and two sets of aunts and uncles. It was stressful and I cannot recall one word of the ceremony, but I do remember when Danny put the ring on my finger. It was a beautiful white gold band with four little diamonds. I was so touched because I knew he was worried about supporting us, and he had spent more then he needed to. It was a loving gesture, and with that ring he was telling me more than words could say.

Later, at my parents house we had cake and ice cream. Photographs captured a laughing Dan and Arlette, but I remember nothing about the reception except Larry and Jack coming into the house still dressed in their fatigues. Their wives had met their bus in a town sixty miles from Lemmon, so they could tell them what was happening back home. The two came in and enveloped me in hugs, and I knew they wished us well. I should have known they would be supportive because in my family we always have made the best of every situation. *Accept what you cannot change, then make the best of it!* This could have been our family motto.

Earlier that week, Danny and I rented an apartment above Nick's Produce. This establishment sold dairy products and baby chicks. In another building nearby they killed cows. What delightful surroundings! The furnished apartment seemed wonderful when we looked at it with our mothers, except it had twin beds. I didn't say a word, but Danny mentioned to the landlord, "We would like a double bed, please." I about died! I can remember my face getting red and I couldn't look at anyone in the room.

The week of the wedding I spent much of my time cleaning this apartment, moving in and arranging our few possessions. It seemed about as real as playing house. It reminded me of the time when Darlene and I had asked the realtor in Lemmon if we could play in this rundown little shack that had a "For Sale" sign on it. The sign said "See Helen C. Tubbs Realtor" – so we did.

I remember going into her little office on Main Street and asking her if we could clean up and play in that tiny house. Incredibly, she reached in her desk and handed us the key! That would never happen in today's world. Everyone would be afraid of someone getting hurt and the potential liability. But no one in Lemmon had <u>ever</u> sued anyone else. It wouldn't have happened then, and would even be a rare thing today in a small South Dakota community.

I remember the excitement as we unlocked the door of this tiny little home and walked through the four rooms. We ran home to get rags and brooms to start cleaning it. Then we asked the local auto body shop for old paint and got lots of leftover colors. We mixed the paints together and proceeded to beautify that dumpy house. Darlene and I cleaned, painted, hung pictures and laid rugs. We furnished the two rooms with boxes and discards, transforming it inside and out into a playhouse fit for two princesses.

There I was, just a few years later, cleaning and painting an apartment, and trying to transform it into something nice. Only this wasn't pretend, this was for real. In a few days this was where Danny and I would live. God help us!

After the wedding reception, most of Danny's relatives came over to look at our apartment. Someone brought refreshments and our first guests ended up staying half the night. They were very nice, fun and funny. It helped to know these good people were part of the new life Danny and I were starting together. There were a lot of new bride and groom jokes, and Danny seemed to enjoy all the banter. Everyone finally left at about three in the morning and we retired. Just a few hours later they were back banging on the door to wake us up for Sunday morning church services.

That was our honeymoon.

Chapter 4

Newlyweds

Married life was a lot like playing house, at least in the beginning. I cooked and cleaned while Danny went to work each day at the lumber yard.

Danny had to report for work at seven o'clock, so like a good little wife, I got up at six each morning and made him breakfast before he left. Our apartment was within sight of the lumber yard. Danny would come home for his coffee breaks and lunch.

In the late afternoon my girlfriends would come over after school and fill me in on the latest gossip. This seemed so strange and even a little sad. I missed school. But as soon as Danny came home my world brightened up. Danny really seemed to enjoy married life. The guy that could party with the best of them, drove too fast and fought too often, became Mr. Domestic. He not only put both feet on the ground, he let them sink in about two feet and take root. When his friends would come over and try to cajole him into going out, he flatly refused. His number one priority was us.

Danny's second worry was money, or rather the lack of it. Money was an ever-looming problem. Danny was making about fifty dollars a week. This barely covered our rent and necessities. There was none left over for extras. Danny worried about what we would do when our clothes wore out. How would we ever be able to buy new things? Here we were with a baby on the way. So when Danny was offered a better paying job with a grocery store in Mobridge, one hundred miles east of Lemmon, we didn't think twice about it.

Leaving Lemmon didn't bother me at all. It was rather exciting to be starting fresh in a new community. Besides we were not completely adrift, Darrell and Kay, and several of Dan's aunts and uncles lived there too. We loaded our few belongings into Dan's car and his parent's car and we were on our way.

In Mobridge, Danny was earning about seventy-five dollars a week. He worked from eight until five, six days a week plus one evening. Sadly, as most of us find out at one time or another, there never is enough money. By the time we moved I was five months pregnant and needed to start seeing a doctor. We did not have insurance so the added money went to pay for this new expense.

While Danny was at work, I watched television and kept busy with housework, cooking and laundry. Laundry was a big chore because we did not have a washer or dryer so I had to walk to the laundromat. We had a car, but I was not old enough to drive. So, I walked.

Walking to the doctor, the grocery store, to visit Kay and to the dreaded laundromat carrying our basket of laundry took up most of my time. Cooking took up very little because we lived mostly on frozen pot pies. This wasn't because I couldn't cook anything else, but because at five for a dollar, that was about all we could afford. I will not eat a frozen pot pie to this day. If we wanted variety, we ate macaroni.

Each day, I looked forward to Danny coming home from work. We were always so happy to see one another. Our time together was spent snuggling in front of our used, forty dollar, black and white television. Some evenings we would visit relatives or go for a little drive. We did not have money to eat out or even take in a movie. In the first five years of our marriage we went to one movie. We absolutely could not afford any extravagance. We are both grateful there were no credit cards available then. It would have been so tempting to use them. But at that time, if a birthday came and there was no money, you made do. If the pantry was bare, you made do. No whims and impulse purchases, but no debt. It was a better way of life in many ways.

Some Sundays we drove the one hundred miles to Lemmon to visit our family. This trip was a trade-off. The cost of gasoline for the trip was equaled by the free meals we would get. Oh, the memory of those delicious meals. Real food! Chicken, mashed potatoes, salads, and even desserts! It sure was a change from the macaroni and pot pies.

Danny and I would talk all the way to Lemmon and back. He would tell me about growing up in Isabel, about walking to Isabel Lake to swim,

24

taking care of chickens, living in the railroad depot and being a farmhand in the summer. Danny still has a way of talking about ordinary things that makes them interesting and adds depth to fond memories. I love to have him share his recollections about when we were dating, or tell me about different vacations we shared. His memory is so good and he remembers details that enhance my memory. I never tire of listening to his voice.

After we had settled in our apartment in Mobridge, Danny wanted me to take instructions in the Catholic Church before our baby was born. I was willing to do this, but I made it perfectly clear that I would only actually join the church if I was convinced it was for me. I began my instructions with an open mind. The lessons were inspiring and I soon found myself eager for the gatherings. It was an emotional and humbling experience the day I was confirmed in the faith that would provide a source of strength in the years ahead.

I went into labor on February 17, 1965. All of my walking during my pregnancy paid off. Without too much misery, I gave birth to a marvelous seven-pound, two-ounce baby boy.

My water broke at about six o'clock that morning. I quickly jumped out of bed, woke Danny and told him this was the day. Then I insisted he go to work. There was so much to do before I went to the hospital. The books all said that with the first birth you have plenty of time so I was determined to use it wisely. First I washed and put rollers in my hair. Then there was the house to clean, and Danny's white work shirts all needed to be ironed. After I finished all of the chores I dramatically called the grocery store to announce to Danny that the time had arrived. (I'm sure I'd seen this on television.)

At the hospital, things progressed very quickly. The doctor arrived just in the nick of time. I gave birth to Curtis with the rollers still in my hair. The nurses had wanted to take them out, but my hair wasn't dry and I had it all planned. I wanted to look great when Danny saw me holding our child for the first time.

My planning could not prepare me for the overwhelming emotion I felt when I saw our son for the first time. This miraculous event made this day the happiest of my life! Curtis Daniel Schweitzer was stunningly beautiful. Danny was so relieved for me and so proud of being a daddy. We were parents! We would do everything right. We would have all the answers. After all, I had watched *Father Knows Best* and *Leave it to Beaver* a lot that year. Oh, happy life – and oh, how young and naïve I was.

Chapter 5

Our Growing Family

Crazy as it sounds, I really did want to pattern our life after the family on the television show *Father Knows Best*. What a great family! They never had problems that couldn't be solved in a half hour. Honesty, security, cleanliness, commitment, involvement, wisdom, warmth and love made for a perfect family. This was for me. So I set out to make our little family as terrific as the Andersons.

Curtis was born on a Wednesday and we took him home from the hospital on a Friday. One of the few things that hasn't changed since the 1960s is that when you don't have insurance hospitals are glad to let you leave.

Danny's parents bought us a used crib. With the crib and the many baby gifts we received we were ready to embark on this new adventure. We drove home put Curtis on the sofa and just looked at him. All he wanted to do was sleep. This was going to be easy!

I'm not blaming Mrs. Anderson, yet it would have been nice if she would have let me know that little Buddy didn't wish to sleep at night. And even though you are getting almost no sleep you still need to cook, clean, make formula, go to the laundromat (in the evenings now) and take care of the baby. Forget the pearls, I was thrilled to get showered and have makeup on before two o'clock in the afternoon. Danny's cutesy little breakfasts were quickly a thing of the past.

The next two years went so fast bringing many changes and several moves. We lived for a short while in McLaughlin, South Dakota, where Dan worked for the same grocery chain as the store in Mobridge. We

26

then transferred to Timber Lake, South Dakota, and eventually back to the original grocery store in Mobridge.

The most profound change during these years was the death of my father. Owen Charles Rafferty died in his sleep at the age of 54. Curtis was just two and Dad had just spent the weekend with us. He entertained little Curtis with rides in his wheel chair. Darlene had graduated from high school by this time and was living with us while working at a bank in Mobridge. Poor Danny had two distraught girls to deal with. This was a terrible blow to our entire family.

Dad had abruptly stopped drinking shortly after our marriage and Mom and us kids were enjoying the wonderful man that was our sober and loving husband and father. With his death, gone were the weekends playing cards or fishing with Dad.

I treasure the memory of Dad and Mom staying with Danny and Curtis for ten days while I was hospitalized for gall bladder surgery. That was something that could never have happened had Dad still been drinking. They stayed another week after I was discharged from the hospital to help me. This was a great time for me. I seemed to really get to know my parents adult to adult during this time. We spent most evenings playing cards and the four of us had fun and many laughs. That time together was a gift from God, I am sure.

Dad died in March; Darlene was married in May; and Danny, Curtis, Scamp (our dog,) and I moved to Aberdeen, South Dakota, in July of 1967. Danny had been offered a sales job, selling and delivering potato chips. The pay was great compared to what we were living on, so we made the big move to the city! Aberdeen was another 100 miles east and the population neared 26,000 people, ten times larger than my hometown. I had my driver's license now but I wasn't sure I could drive in such a metropolis!

At first we rented an apartment, but Danny was eager to get a house because he missed yard work. Soon we found a house to rent, but I hated it! I missed the security and companionship of an apartment full of people. I had made friends with two of the women in our apartment. Both of these friends had children, but one was divorced and the other woman's husband was a prisoner of war in Viet Nam. The three of us would visit as the children played. It was nice having other adults to talk to, and I think of how difficult and lonely it must have been for them not to have husbands at home.

Danny was out of town from early Wednesday morning until late Friday night. It may have been childish, but I was scared in that old, creepy house. Scamp was as big a coward as I was, so the push was on to find something better. It was 1968 and we decided two things: we would buy a house and have another baby. We could not afford a down payment on a house so we bought a mobile home just three months before the second happiest day of my life.

Christa Marie Schweitzer was born on the morning of Christmas Day 1968. The delivery was fairly easy and so was naming her. We honored her and the special day she was born by naming her Christ with an A. This seven-pound fifteen-ounce bundle was the best Christmas present anyone could wish for.

She was just like a little angel. Not only was she gorgeous but she was such a good baby. Curtis thought she was pretty great too. He never showed any jealousy toward her, even letting her use his blanky.

Life at the Anderson's... the Schweitzer's continued to improve. We had two healthy children, wonderful neighbors and friends, Danny had a good job and I was still enjoying my role as wife and mother. Money was still tight, but both Danny and I realized the importance of one of us staying home with the children. Two incomes would have afforded us some luxuries, such as a night out once in a while, yet we were determined to raise our family traditionally.

When Christa was just 14 months old, I realized we were expecting again. Danny and I were not disappointed. Christa was so good that I knew I could handle another baby just fine. Danny was now a sales representative for another food product, Keebler Cookie Company. Because he was just selling and not delivering, he had more time at home. This new job provided a company car. Now we had two vehicles so when Danny was on the road I could shop, take the children to the doctor or go to the park. It was a new freedom for me. We had just purchased a house. Our lives were getting better, our family was growing, and we were happy and excited about all the changes coming our way. Dreams were coming true and we were so blessed.

Chad Raymond was born December 27, 1970. Because he was born on the Christmas weekend, all of our friends who had promised to watch Curtis and Christa were out of town. So Danny drove me to the hospital. Then after coming back in my room twice to kiss me, he went home to be with the children. By now, I knew the key to having babies was concentration, and I had my own method. With Curtis and Christa I had focused on numbers and counting to myself and I automatically started to use this birthing method once again. This time I included a book on my tummy to read between labor pains. My doctor checked me, then left to rest in the doctor's lounge after instructing the nurse to call him when I was dilated to a seven. Shortly thereafter I had an overpowering pushing pain and delivered little Chad while at the same time shouting "NURSE!!!!!"

Baby Chad weighed in at seven pounds, fifteen and a half ounces. I called Danny.

"Well Papa. You have son number two."

Danny was overjoyed and asked if I was, too. Of course, another boy was fine with me. The joy and miracle of another healthy child was supreme.

Very early that morning, Danny came to see Chad and me for a short time while the children stayed in the waiting room. (Children couldn't come into patient rooms at that time.) Danny was taking Curtis and Christa to his parents' in Lemmon so he could work while I was in the hospital. We had insurance and I was staying the full four days! Those days were a peaceful time which I spent bonding with this precious new baby. It was also a good opportunity to rest up before the hard work began at home.

I was happy to come home again and be with Curtis and Christa and Chad. The two older kids loved "their baby." Both wanted to help, hold and be involved in every aspect of new baby life. Bathing him was a family affair with everyone getting a job to do. We all were having fun.

Curtis was now in kindergarten, Christa was just two, and baby makes three. Life quickly settled into a normal routine and Danny and I never dreamed that in a few short months we would be living a nightmare.

Chapter 6

1971: Tragedy Strikes

On Monday, May 3, Chad seemed to be coming down with a cold. In my experience, a cold can spell trouble. I personally have poor lungs and bronchitis is never far behind ordinary cold symptoms. So, when Chad developed a slight wheeze, I took him straight to the pediatrician. The doctor who examined Chad seemed to think I was overreacting.

"There's nothing to worry about, Arlette," he tried to reassure me.

The rest of the day and into the evening Chad was fussy, but when Curtis and Christa went to bed, he fell asleep, too. It didn't last long. All night he fussed and seemed to have a some trouble breathing.

About three in the morning I called the doctor and told him I wanted to bring Chad into the hospital because he couldn't sleep and wasn't breathing normally. He stated emphatically that there was nothing wrong and I should just let him cry himself to sleep. I spent the rest of the night rocking and walking my poor little baby. About six in the morning he finally fell asleep from sheer exhaustion. I too, was exhausted and I was in bed for only a short time before Danny rose to get ready for work.

When Danny came to kiss me good-bye I asked if he had checked Chad. Danny reassured me that Chad was fine. Chad had awakened and Danny gave him his pacifier and the little guy went right back to sleep. It was close to eight in the morning and I was hoping I could get another hour or two of sleep before any of the children woke.

The next thing I knew, Curtis and Christa were both clambering on my bed. They were happy and eager to start the day. I spent a few moments cuddling them before I checking on Chad. One look and I knew he was dead.

What followed felt like an out-of-body experience. It seemed like I was on the outside looking in at the most horrible scene. First I called the operator (this was before communities had 911 service) and told her, "My baby is dead." She asked me to "speak up" but even then I was conscious of Curtis and Christa. I didn't want them to hear me. After I hung up the phone, I hurried them across the street to a neighbor. They both knew something was wrong because I hadn't dressed them and I must have looked shattered.

"What about Chad, Mommy?" Curtis asked.

"The angels took Chad to heaven last night," I said, trying not to cry.

Waiting for the ambulance was agony beyond description. I paced like a crazed animal. When they came, I watched them walk through mud in the front yard as if they were in slow motion. The muddy footprints that materialized as they made their way into Chad's bedroom are forever etched in my memory. Footprints of doom and loss.

The ambulance drivers asked me if I wanted to get dressed and I numbly pulled a denim shift from the closet and slipped it over my head. They asked me about shoes and I just walked out of the house bare-footed. I still have that denim shift in the back of a spare closet. I really don't know why I can't part with it. On rare occasions I look at it and touch it. I still am that shattered young mother, walking barefoot to the ambulance that is carrying her dead baby. I don't want to forget that place and time, and baby Chad.

As I rode in the ambulance to the hospital, I was acutely aware of what was happening, yet it didn't seem like something as awful as this could really be true. It must be a bad dream. The "Oh no, no" that was escaping from my lips was more like a moan. I could hear it as though it were coming from someone else and not me. It came from a place so deep inside that I realized I had never before experienced real pain. Not pain like this. It was as if someone had torn a huge hole in my stomach. Each breath brought pain that was like cold on a raw nerve. The pain was as physical as it was emotional. It was all-consuming and inescapable.

At the hospital, I was put in a room with very large windows and I remember thinking that if I could just walk through those windows and fall to my death I could put an end to this pain. Only the thought of Curtis and Christa kept me from this. Not even the thought of Danny, my soul mate, stopped me. He didn't need me the way the children did. This was one time when my spouse did not come first. Thoughts of Curtis and Christa bounced in and out of my crazed and tormented mind. I knew

31

they were bewildered and would need so much comforting when they realized what had happened to their baby brother. Only their need for me gave me the courage to face life.

The doctor came and wanted me to sign a form permitting an autopsy. I signed. He acknowledged that I had called him in the night and then went on to tell me that this could not have been prevented. Sudden Infant Death Syndrome or crib death could happen even if he himself had been holding Chad.

I did not believe him.

I felt the doctor had let me down. Even worse, I felt I had let Chad down by listening to the doctor's advice instead of to my own instincts.

A nun and a hospital priest came into the room. They wanted to see if there was a relative they could call to come be with me. They looked so desperate when I told them that we had no relatives in Aberdeen. My best friend was Vergene Comes and they decided to call her. Vergene came to the hospital to get me and I really broke down when I saw her. She took me to her house and the parish priest arrived to try to comfort me.

Many people were trying to locate Danny, his main office, the distribution manager and the highway patrol. When they finally contacted him they told him to head back to Aberdeen because something was wrong at home.

When Danny arrived at Vergene's, I met him at the door. Before I could speak he said, "Chad is dead isn't he?"

I nodded my head yes and started to sob. Danny held me and said over and over, that he knew when he got the message to come home that it was Chad. Danny said he had prayed all the way home that Chad was just sick, but in his heart he knew when it wasn't me trying to reach him, that Chad was dead.

Danny wanted to go home to our house immediately. When we got there I didn't think I could go inside. He calmly and patiently coaxed me out of the car. Finally, I put one foot in front of the other and forced myself to walk to the house and go inside. Once in, we just sat on the sofa hardly speaking and not knowing what to do.

The symbolic muddy footprints leading to and from Chad's bedroom kept me transfixed. Those footprints took our baby away, and we would never have him back again.

Every detail up to this point is burned into my mind. The images are as clear today as they were then. Only after that do my memories start to blur. I don't know who called the relatives or when people started to arrive. One moment Danny and I were sitting together on the sofa in the early afternoon. The next thing I recall is that our house was full of people and it was night. Both Grandmothers came to take care of Curtis and Christa.

I later remember being taken to the hospital by Danny and his father for an injection to help me sleep. I'm not certain whose idea this was, or why this was decided. I also remember repeating in my mind, "This was the Lord's will. His will, not ours." I kept praying "His will be done" over and over until I eventually fell asleep.

The next day everyone that had come from Lemmon made the return trip back. We had decided to hold the funeral there. My brother, Jack, worked for the mortician in Lemmon, so when he went back he took Chad's body with him. Jack had come to my bedside and talked to Danny and me about transporting Chad's little body. He could go back to Lemmon and get a hearse to transport Chad's body, or he could take him in his car when he went today. Both of us felt better about Chad's last trip with his Uncle Jack in his own vehicle. We were grateful that Jack was escorting our precious little boy.

Making funeral arrangements for your own child is as difficult a task as can be imagined. Our parents, brothers, sisters and friends surrounded us with love and guidance to keep us going. Within a few days it was all over and it was time to go home and try to face life again.

If ever I questioned my mental stability, this was the period of my life when I truly wondered if I could hold it all together. Each morning meant awakening anew to the pain that was blissfully gone (much of the time) in my sleep. It seemed like I had to remind myself to breathe and to put one foot in front of the other to walk. Nothing came naturally anymore, and trying to make life normal for Curtis and Christa was a challenge.

I went through the motions of being a wife and mom, but I knew I did odd things. When I vacuumed the bedroom where Chad died, I couldn't close the door and be in there while the vacuum was running. When Danny was out of town, I sometimes slept on the floor with Curtis on one side of me and Christa on the other. When I was forced by necessity to go shopping for groceries, I was amazed that people didn't stare at me. I was sure that this gaping wound was visible and that all who looked at me could see how broken I was. When people said "hello" or smiled I was surprised that they thought I was a normal human being whose life was similar to theirs. But my life wasn't like theirs. Their lives were whole and mine was shattered. Couldn't they tell? If someone intruded into my life enough to make small talk they invariably asked how many children I had. My mouth would dully say "two," but my heart would scream "THREE!" Staying sane took so much of my energy.

Danny and I handled Chad's death differently. I wanted to talk with him about it, but he wanted to never talk about it. The one thing we both agreed upon was that I wasn't strong enough to have another baby.

I was twenty-three years old and I needed to have my tubes tied, a radical decision for Catholics. My regular obstetrician was against it. He was worried that I would later regret the decision. Finally I found another doctor to perform the overnight surgery. The only regret I ever had concerning the tubal ligation was guilt because I knew my church did not approve. Eventually I talked to our priest about what I had done and why. He was very understanding and this made me feel much better.

Slowly the days turned into weeks and the weeks into months. Then one day I realized that I had gone a period of an hour or so without thinking of Chad. This time gradually increased until one night after about four years I went to bed and realized that I had not thought of Chad at all that day. I felt guilty. At the same time I knew that the healing was really going to happen and I wouldn't be broken forever.

Life does go on. Life did go on.

Chapter 7

Career & New Opportunities

Chad's death affected our lives in many different ways. It ultimately was the catalyst that put me into the workforce. After Christa started going to school, being a stay-at-home mom began to lose it's appeal. Christa and Curtis were both gone all day and the house seemed very lonely. I wanted to get a job but I had absolutely no work experience and very little education. I tried selling cosmetics door to door, but many of my customers really could not afford the luxuries they were buying. My conscience bothered me when I delivered huge orders and collected money that should have been going for groceries. It was always easy for people to order and difficult for them to pay. The job wasn't for me.

Then I answered an ad to clean motel rooms. This I knew I could do. I was always good at cleaning! Danny was not happy about me going to work. He felt strongly that I should be at home when the kids were. After I assured him that I would not have to be gone while they were home, he reluctantly agreed.

After a few months, I realized many people leave disgusting messes behind when they know someone else has to clean it. After a few revolting encounters, I gave my notice. My life as a working mom was put on a back burner.

A pleasant diversion for our family came in the shape of a used camper trailer. Curtis, Christa, Danny and I would head west to the beautiful Missouri River and camp with Dan's parents, his brother Mike, sister Kay and her family. An assortment of aunts and uncles usually joined us. This was such fun and continued to be a main source of entertainment for many years. We camped nearly every weekend and on many vacations until the kids were teenagers. Many times, my brother Jack, his wife Carol, and their children joined us with their camper. These trips created warm memories of campfires, card games, fishing, rock hunting and the coziness only other campers can understand. Most every evening, the four of us would play card games while enjoying a big bowl of warm popcorn until bedtime.

It was during these years that I began to feel well once more. The scars were there but smoothing out a bit each day. One overpowering aftereffect of Chad's death was my protectiveness of Curtis and Christa. I watched over them with an eagle eye, always calling them closer when they swam and not letting them get too far from our campsite when they fished or hunted for rocks.

This need to know where the children were and if they were safe still continues. Their lives are their own, but I need to be assured that they are well, safe and happy. I am as protective of all my grandchildren as I was Curtis and Christa. My grandchildren laughingly repeat my litany of advice and rules when they want to hike, swim or even ride a bike! Their teasing led me to write a children's book entitled *Grandma Worries About Everything and Grandpa Worries About Nothing.*

A year or so after my pathetic attempt to work outside the home, I decided to do something about my lack of education. Without telling a soul I went to the local college and made arrangements to take a high school equivalency (GED) test. I was told it would require two days of testing and I started the same day I inquired. Not telling anyone gave me the option of never telling anyone, in case I failed the tests. Much to my delight I scored well on the tests and the professor encouraged me to enroll in some college courses immediately. Even though my confidence level had risen considerably with my high school equivalency diploma, I still wasn't secure enough to actually enroll in a college course. We really didn't have the money for that either.

That evening I confided to Danny about my GED. He was so thrilled and proud of me. That was nearly as wonderful as passing the tests. Danny has always had a way of making me feel as though I am the brightest, most capable individual. This is a gift which I realize is coming from a man wearing rose-colored glasses when it comes to me. I hope the tint doesn't ever wear off.

Life wasn't and isn't always perfect. Danny and I have had our arguments. We made mistakes raising the children, but the basic commitment to them and to each other was never in question. Family always came first. Family still always comes first.

The children and I knew we were always first in Danny's life. He would even take us (including the dog) with him on the road many times. When Danny sold potato chips, we would all pile in the front of his truck and away we'd go. Later when he became a sales representative the trips were even better because Danny traveled in a car. This was much roomier and as the children grew, the truck was becoming too small for all of us.

These trips were great fun for all of us. While Danny made his sales calls to the various stores, the children and I would walk around the small communities or visit their parks. In the evenings we might go for a drive, play games or swim at the motel. Combined with eating in restaurants, these outings were almost like being on vacation.

When Christa was about to enter the third grade, I was surprised one summer morning when I got a call from the principal of her school. He wanted to know if I was interested in a job. Still trying to live up to the *Mrs. Anderson/Father Knows Best* image, I was deeply involved in all school activities. This included serving as president of our local Parent Teacher Association. It was through these activities that Mr. Hauge, the children's principal, recognized my efforts and ability to work with children. This prompted the call and the offer. I was thrilled and scared at the same time.

The job was a newly created position, that of a library aide. The next morning I went for the interview. It was overshadowed by the typewriter which loomed on the desk in the library. Leaving high school in the ninth grade, I hadn't typed a single word in my life. That huge machine seemed to be staring at me and intimidating me. It certainly did nothing for my confidence.

Fortunately, Mr. Hauge and Mrs. Valnes (a teacher sitting in on the interview) were convinced that I had something to offer the students. So, I entered into an important phase of my life. I really was a working mother! I felt like shouting, "I AM SOMEBODY!"

The position of library aide was a first for the entire Aberdeen School District. Lincoln School had just been built to replace an outdated and unsafe structure. A lovely library had been designed in the plans and later built.

My new job was to check out and shelve library books, and I worked half days. It was great fun and with each passing day the library got busier. Soon, I was employed full days.

A Schweitzer family portrait from the late 1970s.

The staff at the school was so helpful and encouraging that soon I was offering programs and striving to complement their curriculum with library materials. It was such a joy to work with and read to the students. The teachers continued to bolster my self-confidence with praise and genuine friendship. This was good for my ego, and I loved every minute of my job. Getting paid for it was a bonus.

Another bonus to the job was that Christa and I were at the same school and our schedules were the same. I also had the same days off as the children did, and of course my summers were free. I could work out of the home without feeling guilty. This was splendid!

During the ten years I was at Lincoln School, I observed and learned much about the teaching profession. My admiration for the excellent, dedicated teachers continued to grow, but I also encountered some teachers' techniques on which I knew I could improve. I was getting a valuable education without stepping into a college. I also knew that even though I was treated as an equal by the teachers and the principal, there was a significant difference. I felt inferior because I'd never actually finished high school let alone attended college. This was an embarrassment to me and although no one at the school ever made me feel inferior, I felt that I was. Many of the staff encouraged me to take a class at the college and see how I liked it.

Finally in 1981, with some prodding and much moral support, I enrolled in a psychology class at Northern State University in Aberdeen. I was 33 years old and had a son about to graduate from high school.

The first night at college was traumatic. I felt completely out of my element. I had difficulty finding the right building where the class was being held. When I did locate the building, I blundered into the wrong classroom and I really felt foolish.

I kept asking myself, "What am I doing here?"

There were two reasons I didn't go home – I hate to admit defeat, plus the tuition and book money was spent! I was committed. Eventually I found the right classroom and from the first night I was hooked. I was spurred by my enthusiasm and my love of reading. I read half the textbook the first week. The subject was interesting, the teacher was good and I wanted to succeed! When the semester was over I had earned an "A" and I had the desire to forge ahead.

The next semester I enrolled in two night classes. Then three, then an early morning class in combination with some nights. Then I was taking an early morning class, two night classes, and I also managed to squeeze one in during my lunch hour. My lunch hour class was thanks to the new principal, Mr. Lickfelt. He knew I put in many hours beyond those for which I was paid, so he allowed me the time to get to the college, take my class and be back for the afternoon sessions.

Time flew and I racked up grades and class hours like someone stashing money in a bank. I was the Scrooge of class credits. I was obsessed with getting my degree and had mapped out exactly how many credits I would need and how long it would take me. I listed everything on the back cover of a notebook and I marked off each completed class with relish. College was hard work but also a grand adventure. Soon, I was not only accepted by the younger students but we enjoyed a mutual respect that came from group assignments and humorous bantering. My world was expanding and I was growing in self-confidence too.

Danny was so proud of me as he realized that I was trying hard to be *Super Mom*. It was important to me to keep the house up, attend the kids' functions, and do a good job at my work while going to school. Many nights, I couldn't start my schoolwork until everyone was in bed. Then I would study far into the night. Excitement and commitment kept my energy level high. Curtis and Christa were not little children anymore. They could look after themselves and also help around the house.

All of this was a huge adjustment for Danny. He had come from a traditional home where the man worked and the wife stayed at home. We were a typical couple from the fifties, even though it was the seventies. It was just tradition that I should do the women's work while Danny brought home the bacon.

Super Mom started running low on gas without realizing it.

I arrived home from work one day and was thinking about my night class that started in less then two hours. Danny was reading the paper. He lowered it and asked, "What are you making for dinner?"

I don't remember what I said or how I said it, but it was a turning point in our traditional roles.

Danny started to do more housework and even attempted cooking after that afternoon. We usually shared the housekeeping tasks after that day. Dan mastered all of these skills so well that I, in good-humor, called him "Susie" for Susie Homemaker.

Once, in my distracted enthusiasm for school, I came home while Danny was cooking dinner and sat at the kitchen counter talking. Dan continued to cook, then set the table. We ate and I continued to chatter while he started to clear the dishes away.

Finally, Dan asked, "Are you going to help at all?"

"I just hate to intrude upon another woman's kitchen," I replied with mock sincerity.

Fortunately, Danny's sense of humor is the best of anyone I've ever known. We shared a good laugh while finishing up together.

The Schweitzer family enjoyed a few years of normalcy. It was a busy time with two teenagers in the house. Phones ringing, friends hanging out, activities to attend. Wonderful years. Curtis graduated from high school and started attending the same college I was. The only blight during this time was the death of our beloved dog, Scamp. We had Scamp for eighteen years, and he was such a part of our family and of Curtis' and Christa's lives. His death was a profound loss for us.

In 1983, Curtis was planning to marry Gina Hartford, his high school sweetheart. It seemed like only a moment before, Curtis was walking into the kindergarten classroom. Now here he was, ready to walk down the aisle and take on the responsibility of marriage.

In class I found my mind wandering to what I was going to wear to the wedding. I had to force my thoughts back to genetics or whatever topic we were covering. Our lives never seemed to have a lull.

Gina and Curtis made a gorgeous bride and groom. Dan and I now moved into another stage of our lives realizing our children would soon be on their own. It was an adjustment not having Curtis at home, but we were happy to see him and Gina building their lives together. We saw them frequently even though they were busy with college courses and work.

At Lincoln School it had become the custom to announce major family events by providing a supply of doughnuts in the teacher's lounge along with a note of explanation. My note read, "Our son, Curtis, who we thought might be a priest (many years ago), is instead going to be a Father."

On March 21, 1984, our first grandson Lucas Hartford Schweitzer was born. Gina's parents, Danny and I were in the labor room with the new parents. Christa came in and out. It was a real family affair and excitement ran high. When Curtis carried his son out of the delivery room and handed him to me, I wept with wonder and love.

Danny and I were thrilled to have a grandchild, but as we prepared for bed later that nigh,t my loving spouse turned to me and said, "I can't believe I'm about to go to bed with a Grandma!"

It was wonderful and strange to be a grandparent at thirty-five. It seemed that we had just packed away the high chairs and toys. Here it was time to bring them back out. Gina went back to work and Lucas was lovingly bounced between his only Aunt (Christa), Danny and me, and Gina's parents. This was a great arrangement because the extra love and stimulation from his extended family, coupled with that from his devoted mommy and daddy, made for one happy and bright boy.

It was while I was rocking Lucas on a warm August day in 1984, that the phone call came that changed our lives.

Chapter 8

Hope at the Mayo Clinic

Soon after Christa was diagnosed with Mayer-Rokitansky-Kuster-Hauser Syndrome, it was time to start another school year. I was still dazed by the diagnosis. I shared this information with only two or three close friends. It was a private matter and I felt that Christa would tell those she wished to tell and that I didn't have the right.

The 1984-85 school year was a crazy, hectic one. My sister Darlene's husband died that August. She moved into an apartment across the street from Danny and me to try to cope with his death. My mother had a third open heart surgery. My asthma (that developed when I was twenty-seven) continued to worsen. I had several severe attacks that sent me to the emergency room. All of this plus Danny's colitis, which had been dormant since high school, came back with a vengeance.

That year stands out as one of the most trying years of our married life. It was as though nothing could go right. We had one blow after another and I knew that if I let go and started to cry, I might never stop. The stress and strain affected my grades at Northern, and the pride I took in getting A's and B's slipped as I missed classes due to Mom's health and my asthma.

I continued to work full time while carrying a weighty college load. Combining this with all of the outside pressures made me eager for the school year to end. For the first time since I started my job at the school I wondered if I could handle everything.

In the spring on 1985, I made the difficult decision to quit my aide job at Lincoln School in order to attack college classes unencumbered. It was wrenching for me to leave my dear friends and a job I loved, but I knew it was time. Danny and I both knew we would miss my salary after ten years, yet we also knew I couldn't get all the classes I needed by attending only nights and summers. School ended on June 4th. On June 5th this thirty-six-year-old grandmother of Lucas was a full-time student.

As always, when I start a project I want to work straight through to completion. College was no different. Now that I had set my goal, I took as many classes as the school would allow each semester. I was determined to get it over so Danny and I could move forward with our lives. I worked even harder at school, determined to complete all the necessary courses in one year so I could start earning money once more. I planned to cram nearly sixty credits in one school year and begin teaching in the fall of 1986!

Dan's parents, recognizing our sacrifice and financial hardship, generously offered to pay for my tuition that final year. This was a wonderful gift and it meant more to me than they could ever know.

That same summer, it was time to return to the University of Minnnesota to make a decision about how to deal with Christa's Mayer-Rokitansky-Kuster-Hauser Syndrome. Instead, we decided to get another opinion at the Mayo Clinic in Rochester, Minnesota. An appointment was made for late August and the three of us were off once more. The trip to the clinic was not somber like our first trip to Minnesota, but hopeful. We were eager to get another opinion on this rare syndrome.

The Mayo Clinic is as awesome as it is attractive. The grounds are beautifully manicured and everything seems so bright and clean. What exists today is the legacy of the Mayo family, a physician father and his two physician sons, and of the visionary Catholic nuns who founded the first hospital in Rochester. Seed money for the new hospital was actually provided by a number of communities in the region, including cities in both of the Dakotas.

The Doctors Mayo were early subscribers to sterile technique and pioneered advances in surgery that transformed medical practice in the late 19th and 20th centuries. They realized that the profession of medicine would require thoroughly trained practitioners, so they openly invited surgeons from around the world to Rochester to study and observe new surgical techniques. These teaching sessions were referred to as the "Mayo Clinics," from which the current name derives. In addition to surgical advances, the Mayo Clinic also became associated with advances in clinical diagnosis. Today, people from all over the world can be found in the waiting rooms of the Mayo Clinic. It is a place of anticipation and hope.

Christa and I were ushered in to meet Dr. William Ory, a gynecologist specializing in infertility. After he examined Christa, he gave us the news we had been praying for. Physically, he could see no reason for any reconstructive surgery. Christa was normal, just smaller than most girls her age. When the time came, a loving, gentle husband could do as much as any surgeon.

We were elated and summoned Danny to hear this good news. As for the absent uterus, Dr. Ory explained there was nothing he could do.

"I wish there was a way I could donate my uterus so it could be transplanted in Christa," I said. "After all, I'm certainly not going to be using it any more."

Dr. Ory looked at me quizzically. "How old are you, Arlette?" he asked.

"I'm thirty-six."

It was if a light went on for all of us at once.

"That presents us with another possibility," he said.

Christa, Danny and I realized what he was thinking and we fairly

My graduation day in 1986. I'm show here with Danny and my grandson Lucas.

44

danced around the little examining room as we realized what this could mean. After Doctor Ory calmed us down a bit we asked if he would try the procedure when the time came. He agreed.

"I don't want you to get your hopes too high," Doctor Ory cautioned. "What we're thinking about has never been done before."

A mother and daughter teaming up to give birth to a child would break new ground. Dr. Ory would also need to present the idea to the ethics board at the clinic to obtain approval when the time came.

The trip home was one of intense excitement. Danny, Christa and I chattered the miles away. We had planned to stop for the night instead of driving straight to Aberdeen, but we were all too stimulated to think about sleeping. Sometime during all this conversation, Danny said that it was after midnight and we were celebrating our twenty-first anniversary. We both agreed that we couldn't have received a better anniversary gift. Christa was not going to need surgery and we had been given the gift of hope!

I needed to suppress my excitement and concentrate on the remainder of the school year at Northern State. The academic load was really taxing, but it was paramount that I achieve my goal. In order to graduate the following summer, I couldn't deviate from the plan. I couldn't drop one class or miss a single credit. It was go, go, go.

With the help and support of my family, I graduated from Northern State University in August 1986 with a major in Library Media and a second major in Elementary Education. When the dignitaries called, Arlette Rafferty Schweitzer, one ecstatic, proud, tired lady – gowned and capped for the occasion – danced onto the stage for her diploma. It really should have read, *Daniel R. and Arlette R. Schweitzer* because Danny certainly earned it, too. We had achieved this together!

Chapter 9

Family Discussion

My goal to have a teaching job by the fall of 1986 did not material-ize. Graduating in August and hoping to begin to teach that same month was grandiose. I knew it, but I had all my hopes in one basket called Lincoln School.

There was an opening for a second grade teacher at Lincoln School where I had worked. I was crushed when the current principal did not choose to hire me. Nearly all the teachers had put in a good word for me and they felt bad, too. It felt like such a slap in the face after being a loyal and dedicated employee of that school for ten years. I realized I wasn't an experienced classroom teacher, but I felt I deserved a chance, and this was a total letdown. Not getting a teaching position changed the plan I had for the future. I hadn't really considered any alternatives, and part of my disappointment stemmed from realizing my own shortsightedness.

Usually, when I get something in my head, it goes the way I want. I'm not sure if that has been due to the power of positive thinking, stubborn persistence or just plain dumb luck. Even if I appear unsettled externally, internally I have faith things will work out. So, this early career disap-pointment really humbled me. Not only did that loss hurt my ego but we were counting on a teaching job to help compensate for the income lost while I finished my education. Of course, some of the best opportunities for growth come from learning how to handle our failures.

Fortunately, I received an offer to tutor students in kindergarten through the sixth grade at another elementary school in Aberdeen. The pay was the same as a beginning aide, yet the district wanted someone with a degree in education. This desperate soul filled the bill. I was very grateful to the principal of that school for giving me the opportunity to prove myself as an educator. I was determined to show Mr. Martell that he had made a wise choice.

I worked hard and lay awake nights dreaming of ways to help my students. Tutoring was a wonderful experience and I cared deeply for the kids that came to me for extra help. It became a personal challenge to make their study time interesting and rewarding. Ultimately, I was the one rewarded with students who worked hard for me and achieved goals of which we could all be proud.

The key to helping the students realize their potential was to first discover what they did best, build their confidence, and then work on areas where they struggled. Once they recognized that everyone has weaknesses and we ALL have strengths and talents, the rest was a breeze.

Every teacher I know gives students one hundred and ten percent of what they have to give. I did the same. My students got all I had to give and it paid off. I was happy and proud of them, and of myself.

The following school year I was offered a first grade teaching position in yet another elementary school in our community. Once again I was surrounded by warm and talented teachers. It seems that most of the people in education are caring, sharing individuals who are willing to reach out and share ideas and advice. I would be lying if I said there were no spoiled apples in the barrel, but those are few, thank God. I am extremely proud to be a part of the education community.

Danny, Christa, my mother and sister, Marlis, all helped to decorate and transform the small library room that was to become my classroom. After everything was ready and I was all alone, my first order of business was to thank God and ask Him to guide me to be the best teacher for the students in my charge. I prayed that I would truly be a teacher, not just because my diploma said I was one. An empty desk in the classroom reminded me that He was there, guiding me every day.

My first class of students will hold a special place in my heart for the rest of my life. What a thrill to see them grasp the concepts of reading, adding numbers, and telling time. To watch their little faces as I read to them and to feel their warm hugs throughout the day were valuable rewards. Those students touched my life and I hope and believe I touched theirs.

Once again, Danny took pride in my work. Often, when I was correcting papers or writing lesson plans, he and Christa would come to my classroom window, tap, and hold up a sack with our dinner. The three of us would sit around a small table and share our day. Christa was working for Danny as a merchandiser for Keebler Company, as well as attending school. Both she and Curtis had helped their Dad for years, but now Keebler had actually hired her and she was Danny's right hand man. They worked together, lunched together, and Dan liked to tell everyone that Christa bossed him around.

Life was good and only got better with the birth of our second grandson, Clay Curtis Schweitzer. Clay was born November 9, 1987. He gave us all a scare by becoming tangled in the umbilical cord during the last stages of labor. Christa and I prayed outside of the operating room door when his birth became an emergency caesarean section. He was a healthy eight pound boy but poor Gina was asleep for some time after Clay's birth and missed those first precious minutes of his life. Curtis divided his time between Gina's bedside and visiting Clay under the lights in the nursery. For the first four hours or more of Clay's young life, I was bent over his isolette rubbing his tiny legs and arms. I talked to him the entire time, telling him how much he was loved. It was precious time and I wanted him to feel the family's love for him until his Mommy was awake to give him her love.

Danny and I loved Grandson Number Two as much as Grandson Number One. We were determined to treat the boys the same and tiny Clay got to stay overnight at Gramma and Grampa's on Thursday and Saturday nights, just as Lucas did. Curtis and Gina graciously, and sometimes gratefully, shared the boys with us. They lived in a house just four blocks from ours and this made it convenient for them to drop the kids at our house on the way to work. In the winter when I worked they needed to go to day care, but whoever was free first picked them up. Usually it was Danny, but Christa and I also were blessed with this delightful job many times. Gina ached to be a full-time mom. She often expressed that it was unfair that she was the villain who took the children to daycare, while we got to be the heroes who picked them up. Because of our varied, schedules the two boys spent very little time at day care.

Christa was devoted to her nephews. She often gave up her free time to watch them. When they were at our house, she pitched in bathing and caring for them. I knew that Curtis' and Gina's joy in being parents did not give Christa pangs of jealousy, but I'm sure she experienced pangs of wistfulness.

Outwardly, Christa seemed to have put her medical problems on a shelf as Dr. Heinemann suggested. Occasionally, we would mention the future and the possibility of me carrying a baby for Christa. She would even kid me about keeping in shape for things to come.

Danny and I talked about Christa's situation more, especially when we were traveling to out of town meetings. Long drives make for the best conversations. I sensed that Danny wasn't completely sold on the idea of me trying to carry a child for Christa. Sometimes I felt he was just pacifying me with conversation when I would bring it up, hoping that it wouldn't have to be a reality. Nearly all the relatives were pooh-pooing the notion. If Danny also had reservations, I wanted him to say so out loud.

Finally, one evening while we were driving he blurted everything out.

"I really don't think this is a good idea," he said. "Frankly, I only went along with it because I thought it wasn't possible."

I was stunned.

Danny proceeded to tell me he felt Christa and I would eventually forget about it as Christa dealt with her diagnosis. "I figured it was simply part of the healing but not something you should go through with."

"Why exactly do you feel we shouldn't do this?" I pressed.

"I'm really worried about what it would do to your health, Arlette. You've had a number of asthma attacks that have scared me. Aren't there times when you're using a breathing machine four to six times a day? Aren't you on steroids and other medication?"

Danny went on and I realized he had put a lot of thought into this. "Haven't you been rushed to the emergency room dozens of times?"

Along with his fears that my health would be in jeopardy, Danny was concerned that Christa and I were in for a big disappointment.

"I think you believe you're actually going to be able to do this," he said, "and I don't want either of you to get hurt.

"Finally, if you actually are able to go through with this surrogacy thing, I'm worried you'll be too attached to the child and not want to let go."

That really took me by surprise. I thought Danny knew me better than that and had more faith in me. Still, it gave me pause. Would I really have a tough time letting go? I was convinced I wouldn't.

Danny and I realized this conversation was too serious to have while he was driving, so we pulled over to the side of the road and continued. I countered that I knew I would not be unduly attached to Christa's child.

"When the time comes, this child will be Christa's baby, not mine. I'll love this child just like I love our other grandchildren.

49

"I look at this like I look at being an organ donor. If Christa needed a kidney, I would give her one of mine. I know you would give her a kidney if she needed one of yours. Well, Christa needs a uterus," I said. "I can't give her mine, but I can do the next best thing.

"If I could physically donate my uterus to Christa it would be used for the same thing. It would be used to grow and nourish her baby."

If it was so easy for me to see, why was it so inconceivable to everyone else?

Danny and I talked for a long time that evening, but we processed through our concerns. Danny was still worried about my health, but he agreed that if my allergy doctor, Dr. Luzier, said it was acceptable he would support my decision.

As I mentioned, relatives on both sides of the family had reservations about our plan. The entire family knew and felt terrible about Christa's syndrome. They all were aware of Christa's natural maternal instincts, yet they seemed to think that my carrying babies for her was a pipe dream. Whenever the subject was brought up most of them would politely listen, then change the subject. They were thinking so loudly I could almost hear them saying "Yeah, yeah, yeah."

My mother didn't mince any words though. She told me what she thought straight out.

"Arlette, you are too old to consider going through with something like this. Christa isn't even married so you're going to be even older when she actually is ready to start a family," she said. "Considering your asthma I also don't think it's a smart idea. There are just too many risks."

Danny's parents wouldn't talk about it at all. Even when we actually started to go to the University of Minnesota Hospital for the preliminary checkups, they never once asked how things were going. They seemed to think that if it was never discussed, it would go away. I believe they were nervous about what they would tell people.

Of course, avoidance really isn't in my nature. I would bring the subject up among the family because I wanted them to get used to the idea. I wanted everything openly discussed before the time arrived when Christa actually was ready to start a family. It seemed that mountain would be a lot easier to climb if we worked through any family conflicts in advance. I wanted the air clear. When the time came, for Christa's sake and my own health, I didn't want any distractions, upheaval, stress or shocked relatives causing us distress.

Our open supporters were few. My sister, Darlene, and my sister-in-law, Brenda, were the only ones willing to go out on that limb. The rest were either too worried or just plain uncomfortable.

Not that anyone could have changed my mind. Christa and I had our light at the end of the tunnel and we were heading for it. Like everything else in my life, I could visualize the end result. We just had to figure out the path that would lead us there.

Chapter 10

Bridging the Distance

When Clay was two years old, Curtis was transferred to Rapid City, South Dakota. This lovely Black Hills community is nearly three hundred fifty miles from Aberdeen. Curtis, like his Dad, had always wanted to live in the Black Hills of South Dakota. We had often vacationed there and my two brothers who lived there always exalted the virtues of "the Hills."

The area is breathtakingly beautiful, with aromatic pine-covered mountains, clear lakes and picturesque streams. The climate in the Black Hills is also much less severe than on the open plains. We were happy for Curtis and proud of his promotion, but Danny and I knew we were going to miss them very much. Curtis and Gina would benefit from this move – but did they HAVE to take the children?

When moving day came, and the truck with all their belongings pulled away, I felt the most wrenching loss I had known since Chad's death. Danny and I enjoyed grandparenthood so much and we knew the boys benefitted from the relationship, too. Danny and I had a difficult time adjusting. Danny was used to taking the two boys with him everywhere like the park, the doctor, and to my school. Our house was a home away from home for them, filled with books, toys, a sandbox in the yard and a child's pool. The boys helped me cook, clean and even paint. Oh, the patience a grandparent has. We doted on them and yet, like their parents, expected and taught good behavior. We were not above giving them a swat on the behind if necessary. Doting did not mean spoiling.

The toys were put away, the kiddie pool went into the shed and we tried to bandage our wounded hearts.

We accepted focused on the positive aspects of the kids' move. Gina was going to be a stay-at-home mommy. This was her longtime wish and we were all pleased for her and the boys. She finally got to enjoy many of the things she had missed while she was working. It is always an adjustment to lose one income, but Gina and Curtis felt the gain for the children was worth the financial sacrifice. You can always get that second car or buy a dishwasher, but you will never buy back those childhood years.

Gina and Curtis were expecting their third child later that year, and we were all thrilled when boy number three came along. Cole Mathias was born on December 20, 1988. Danny, Christa and I went to Rapid City soon after his birth and we fell in love once more. Cole was as beautiful as the other two boys had been, with lots of dark hair and big brown eyes. The boys all have their Daddy's and Grandpa's dimples and cleft chin, too.

The trip to Rapid City became routine for Danny, Christa and me, especially when Curtis and Gina purchased a unique old log home shortly after Cole's birth. We went five weekends in a row in the spring of 1989, helping them to paint, wallpaper and finally move. We enjoyed helping them and they needed the extra hands. It is amazing to realize that your child has become an adult and a respected friend whose company you enjoy. While child rearing is wonderful, this phase of life brings a relationship that is every bit as wonderful and rewarding.

It was not unusual for us to talk on the phone for several hours, several times a week. We would talk to Gina and Curtis first and catch up on the events in their lives. Then we would talk to each of the boys. Often we would read them stories and sing their favorite songs on the phone. Each child got to talk as long as he needed. The money spent on telephone bills could have paid for a cruise, but the enjoyment we got from these calls could not be compared. We wouldn't have traded those precious minutes with them for a lifetime of trips.

One decision we made when Curtis and Gina moved was that we would never be a burden when we went to visit. We planned to go often and we did not want it to be a pain for them financially or physically. So from day one, we set up the rule that we would bring or buy the meals when we came to visit. That way, our entire time there could be fun and spontaneous, and Curtis and Gina wouldn't have to entertain us. We could go to the park, to the woods, or just plain loaf and not spend all the time in the kitchen. We would grab burgers, or cold meats and cheeses. Sometimes I brought family favorites from home. This worked out great for all of us and we were able to enjoy time together, instead of getting stressed out or imposing on Gina and Curtis.

Chapter 11

Christa and Kevin

Christa continued her job with Keebler after she graduated from high school and started college. Her job as a merchandiser was to put the Keebler products that Danny sold on the shelves in some of the larger stores. Christa and Danny often worked side by side. Many evenings they would share the day's events with me.

One evening Danny mentioned that he felt the new assistant manager at one of the grocery stores had his eye on Christa. Christa stated emphatically, "He better not because, he is married!"

Danny went on to say that he was not married. "I heard he *was* married. He apparently got married very young, but it didn't work out."

Over the next few weeks a friendship developed, and soon Christa and Kevin Uchytil were an item.

One night after Christa and Kevin had been out on a date, Christa returned and solemnly told her Dad and me that she had something important to discuss with us. I put on my robe and the three of us went into the kitchen.

Christa busied herself tidying the counter while she spoke.

"You know that Kevin was married before," she said.

We nodded

"Well, Kevin also has a young son."

"I see. How do you feel about that?" I asked her.

"I guess I was wondering how you would feel about that," Christa responded.

If Danny and I didn't know before, we realized then that Kevin and

Christa were getting serious about one another. We both assured Christa that if she cared deeply for Kevin and he had a son, then that son would be a bonus. We wanted Christa to choose someone who could make her happy. If Kevin were that someone, then we would be happy, too. Another boy in the family would be a welcome addition.

Neither Danny nor I doubted that we could love this little boy we'd never met. Christa went on to explain that she and Kevin were not talking marriage yet, but that they were being very open with one another. I guess they were both testing the water. Each of them had personal pieces of their lives to reveal. Christa had shared with Kevin that her dream to be a mother would not come true in the conventional way. As Christa said later, "If he isn't the type of man who can understand, then I want to know before either of us gets hurt."

One afternoon that fall, while I was working late in my classroom, Christa and Kevin came tapping at the window. They wanted to know if Danny and I would come to dinner with them that evening at seven. Later, as Danny and I were driving to the restaurant I predicted, "They are going to ask us for our permission to marry."

"I think you're getting ahead of yourself, Arlette," Danny replied.

"I could tell by the sparkle in both of their eyes when they stopped by the school this afternoon that something is up," I countered.

We met Kevin and Christa at the restaurant. After we had ordered our meal, Kevin took a deep breath. In a sweet and old fashioned way he turned to Danny and said, "I would like to ask you for your daughter's hand in marriage. I pledge that I will always treasure Christa and love her."

The hope and anticipation were evident on both their faces. After keeping them in suspense for a moment, Danny gave his approval. Kevin was visibly weak with relief. We ordered champagne to toast the occasion and had a lovely meal. We ended the evening with the two of them coming to our house so that Christa could call Curtis and Gina, her grandparents and some aunts and uncles. It was so fun and exciting.

Because Christa was and is special to many of her aunts, uncles and cousins, Kevin faced some daunting scrutiny. My sister Darlene's boys always said they were going to find someone just like Christa when they got married. Naturally, they and everyone else wanted assurances that Kevin really was a knight in shining armor. Of course, the advantage of being accepted into this tightly knit family was that Kevin and his son, Justin, would be included and loved as much as the rest of the clan. We couldn't have been happier if we had picked him ourselves.

Christa always was a sensitive and thoughtful girl. Her priorities were always straight and she was considerate of us and others. It helped that when she went to high school she was surrounded by friends with similar values and structure. All of her friends' parents were strict and involved people, and this made all of our job a bit easier. Christa never spoke unkindly about any of the kids at her school and she never expressed jealousy or "cattiness." She seemed to have gleaned the best qualities from her parents and had sloughed off the less the admirable ones. We were proud of her, and we were sure that Kevin was just as proud and pleased to have won her heart.

Christa and I began planning for the wedding. The date was tentatively planned for the following August, nearly one year away. This was a fun and exciting time for us. We spent every free moment at bridal shops, party shops and pouring over bridal magazines.

Danny and I, always conservative by nature and necessity, planned to splurge on our only daughter. We wanted to give her the best wedding possible. Every detail was important to us, and the year went by quickly as we ordered, booked and scheduled for the incidental side of the wedding.

The sacramental side of the wedding was not going as smoothly. Even though Kevin was not Catholic and had not been married in the Catholic Church, his first marriage had to be annulled if he and Christa were to marry in the Church. Christa and Kevin were completely immersed in church marriage instructions, meetings, forms and more meetings trying to have the annulment completed before the planned wedding date.

We had been hasty setting a date before the annulment. This put a strain on the priests involved as well as all of us. The priests could give us no assurance that the marriage would be annulled. The annulment process is long, complicated and involves many people. Our parish priest cared about us as part of his personal flock yet he knew that the red tape was sticky. He felt caught in the middle and I felt terrible about putting him in that spot. I called the office of the Bishop and Chancellor trying to speed the process along, but one cannot pressure the Church bureaucracy.

Christa's dream wedding included walking down the aisle of Sacred Heart Catholic Church, where she had been baptized and confirmed. Both she and Curtis (and Gina too) had attended and graduated from Catholic schools. The church was, and is, an integral part of all our lives. We all fervently prayed that the annulment would come through, and in time!

The wedding announcements read August 19, and the first week in August I was still on the phone to the diocese office hoping we could express mail, necessary papers. Christa and Kevin were still traveling to meet people designated by the church to work with them about this matter. The stress was peaking!

Chapter 12

A Few Hitches Before the Wedding

Danny was more stressed out than even I realized. Like the rest of us, he was worried that the annulment would not come through in time. Coupled with the fact that he was not only "losing" his daughter, but his right hand helper at work, he was under a lot of pressure. In his usual style, however, he was trying to be a rock for the rest of us.

On August 12, just one week before the wedding, Danny and I were enjoying a beautiful summer day. We received the news that the Church had granted Kevin's annulment the day before and we were happily preparing for the relatives who would arrive in a few days. We joked, laughed, made love, and worked our way through the day and into the night.

At about eleven that evening Danny shouted that he needed me to come upstairs right away. I coyly shouted back, "What do you want now? Whatever it is, it better be good."

I ran up the stairs and headlong into a scene from a horror movie. As wide as Danny could open his mouth, blood was pouring out. He was leaning over the toilet stool and could not even talk. I dialed *911* and prayed as I talked to the woman taking my call. I was nearly in shock myself from the sight, and I was certain at the rate that Danny was losing blood that he would die shortly.

Within moments, I could hear the ambulance. Two wonderful men came to help Danny. They got him into the ambulance. I can't believe I had enough wits about me to get the pets in, close up the house, grab my keys and follow behind them. They were going slowly at first as they were dealing with the torrent of blood that quickly filled then ran over the containers in the vehicle. I was right on their tail, praying the entire way. I begged God to let Danny live. In the hospital emergency room I found him, blood-soaked from his nose to the bottom of his feet. It was a shock just to look at him. The good news was that he had quit vomiting. He was white and weak, and worried about me and the wedding!

Our doctor, Dr. Janusz, was very comforting when he came to see us. I immediately felt more calm because he was not only a wonderful doctor, but a man of obvious faith. He explained that an ulcer had eaten though and ruptured an artery in Danny's stomach. Danny would need an immediate transfusion because he'd lost so much blood. We worried about the possibility of Danny contracting the AIDS virus or other bloodborne illness, but there was not time to take blood from a family member. We knew some blood screening was going on at that time, but everyone in the country also knew about Ryan White and how that innocent young man was infected with the virus. It was an immediate concern, but fortunately our local blood supply proved safe.

Danny was admitted to the intensive care unit of the hospital and I was handed a bag of bloody clothes. After seeing him settled and stabilized, I went home to check on the pets and wash those awful items. I took a few moments to sit on our sofa to calm myself and to pray in the quiet of our home. As I looked around, I realized that nothing mattered except Danny getting well. The house was just a house; the furniture was just stuff; the wedding was an event, not all-important.

I took a deep breath, grabbed an afghan and my rosary and left for the hospital. Danny was pretty miserable with tubes in his nose and IVs in his arms, yet he told me to go home and sleep. I was not about to leave the hospital. It was an interminable wait until morning when I could call the kids. Christa was in Iowa for the weekend, and of course, Curtis and family were in Rapid City. I knew as soon as they heard they would rush home and I didn't want them on the road in a panic.

Waiting for news about Danny's condition was good for only one reason. It put things back in perspective. Before Danny's collapse, details of the wedding and seeing that everything went perfectly were the most important things on my mind. Now, nothing mattered except his health. It's amazing how your whole attitude can be changed in just a matter of minutes. My life had included many jolts in the past, but seeing Danny so vulnerable, especially when he was always so healthy and decisive, left me subdued and frightened.

At about seven in the morning, I reached Curtis and Gina in the Black

Hills and explained the facts as I knew them. They were extremely upset and I implored them to drive carefully. Gina called her parents after they talked to me and asked them to come to the hospital to be with me.

Curtis and Gina were upset that I had been alone all night. I had not been alone. God stayed by my side as I used this time to pray, reflect and think in the hospital chapel when I could not be with Danny.

Christa, Curtis, Gina and the boys arrived within minutes of each other. Danny's brother, sister and parents also made the trip to see him that day. Everyone was shocked to see him looking so white and so weak. He had never before been admitted to a hospital, or even missed a day of work.

Danny remained in the intensive care unit for four days. During that time, I only left the hospital to shower and change clothes. I could go in to see him for ten minutes every other hour and I didn't want to miss a minute. The bleeding was stopped without surgery and Dr. Janusz put Danny on medication for the stomach ulcer. He was dismissed from the hospital two days before the wedding, and we all rejoiced!

The wedding day arrived and we were like bees swarming in a hive trying to get ready for the occasion. Curtis and Gina were both part of the wedding party as were all three of their boys. There we were getting tuxedos on Danny, Curtis, Lucas, Clay and eight-month-old Cole. It was

A family portrait with Curtis holding Cole, Gina, Lucas and Clay at St. Mary's Church, Aberdeen, on Christa and Kevin's wedding day.

a task, but did they look wonderful! Kevin's son, Justin, was ring bearer. Lucas was candle bearer and Clay carried up two roses. Cole just looked good.

Christa looked just like a princess in her wedding gown and Kevin looked like a knight in a white tuxedo. The reception, dinner and dance went as planned. Danny was pale, but so very handsome, and we even danced one dance.

Christa and Kevin had reserved the honeymoon suite at a local motel. The next morning, when they when arrived back at our house, I was at the bottom of the steps and they were in the foyer. I looked up at Christa and put both my hands out with a shrug as if to ask, well? She smiled over Kevin's head and gave me a thumbs-up sign. Dr. Ory's prediction was right.

That day, we served brunch for several relatives including Kevin's parents. As is done per South Dakota tradition, we all shared the joy as Kevin and Christa opened their wedding gifts. Shortly after, the bride and groom departed for a honeymoon in Florida. After all the guests had gone, the house was strangely quiet. Danny and I were a bit melancholy as we realized that for the first time since the early months of our marriage, twenty five years earlier, it was once more just the two of us. We had reached another passage in this fleeting journey of life.

Christa and Kevin's wedding portrait. Kevin's parents Jim and Rosie Uchytil are on the right.

Chapter 13

A Family Plan

Christa and Kevin made their first home in Sioux City, Iowa. Kevin had been promoted and transferred there shortly before the wedding. They rented a house, and Danny and I traveled to see them once a month. We also went to Rapid City, once a month to see Curtis and company. Our phone bills soared again after Christa left home, because we talked with her frequently.

Many parents experience "empty nest syndrome" after their last child leaves. I think this happened more to Danny than to me. The Lord had blessed me with a new career opportunity, thus giving my mind much to gnaw on.

I applied for, and was offered the position of librarian at one of the junior high schools in our city. Books were my first love. When the job was announced, I eagerly applied and got an interview. Danny was disappointed that I would be leaving the classroom. He was very proud of my being a teacher and he felt I made a difference in some of the young lives in our community. Still, he encouraged me in this new endeavor.

It was with regret that I left my little ones, but I also realized that I was ready for a change. Teachers not only work late into the night correcting papers and planning for the next day, they lie in bed thinking about the children that have so many problems in their young lives. My heart ached for the six-year-olds who did not want to go home at the end of the day. Six-year-olds would ask me to "please take my artwork home" because no one at their house would look at it anyway. Six-year-olds came to school with no breakfast. No one had helped them dress and no one had bothered to kiss them good bye. Yes, there were plenty of children from good, solid, stable homes, but thoughts of these others stayed with me day and night. This new position would be more stable and emotionally less draining. The change would be good for me.

Life settled into a routine after Christa's marriage. I practically lived at school, rearranging the library to fit my personality and philosophy. More important, I wanted to make the library a welcoming and stimulating place for the students. It was exhilarating work! The changes were dramatic and satisfying. The challenge of a new position made the school year fly. Once again, I enjoyed meeting and making friends with my new colleagues.

When Danny wasn't at his job, he was helping me move books in the library. If I left the library and he was still working, I would find him and help him at the stores. New challenges, new faces, and a new environment left little time to ponder our empty nest. And of course, the phone calls and visits helped!

Having your children leave home is bittersweet. You miss them and their activities, yet the newfound freedom has a lot to commend it. Danny and I were able dine out more frequently. We were free to come and go as we pleased and we could leave for a day or a weekend on a moment's notice. It was like the honeymoon period we never had. We were able to grow in our relationship and enjoy one another's company in new ways.

Danny and I were both in our forties with the freedom most married couples enjoy in their twenties. As usual, we seem to enjoy everything in reverse order from our cohorts' lives. Having children when most people our age were still in school. Having grandchildren when our friends were having children. Now we had an empty nest when most our age were still going to Little League games. It seemed strange to many, yet it was typical for us.

What was to come next was neither typical nor characteristic of this small-town, unassuming, ordinary South Dakota family.

When Christa and Kevin had been married for about a year-and-a half, they decided it was time to try to start a family. None of us knew how long it would take. Because we would have to employ an extraordinary method, we were certain it would be longer than the usual nine months.

Christa made an appointment with Doctor Ory at the Mayo Clinic for June 6, 1990. As long as we were going to this world renowned clinic, I convinced Danny to have his colon checked at the same time. I am always hoping that something new will be discovered to put his ulcerative colitis into remission. Doctor Janusz helped secure an appointment for Danny on June 5. Perfect! Christa's appointment was a consultation appointment. We wanted Doctor Ory to go over the plan with us and explain what would be involved, as well as the time frame for this untried procedure.

I promised Danny that before I proceeded with this venture I would get the doctor's approval concerning my asthma. Before our Mayo trip I made an appointment to see Doctor Luzier, my asthma and allergy doctor. Doctor Luzier had brought me a long way in the treatment of this affliction. When he first arrived in Aberdeen three years earlier, I was on heavy doses of asthma medications and steroids. Plus, I was using a breathing machine every four hours. I was making several trips a year to the emergency room at the hospital, and I had been admitted to the hospital so many times I wouldn't let them print my name in the list of admissions in the newspaper any more. It was embarrassing.

Now, after being under Doctor Luzier's care, I was down to one pill a day and two allergy shots each week. I felt great and I hadn't been in the hospital for over two years. The breathing machine, a nebulizer, was still a big part of my life. I needed to use it four times a day and often at night. I considered this a mere inconvenience, and I tried to use my nebulizer time wisely by riding an exercise bicycle, listening through a headset to the golden oldies, with a mouthpiece breathing in medicine. What a sight I was. I looked like a creature from outer space!

For a time, I had resigned myself to the idea that I would always use this apparatus, and I had gotten used to it. After living always short of air, it was merely an inconvenience. But now the stakes were higher. What impact could this have on my health and more importantly the baby's? Could I, or should I try to carry Christa's baby while I was on the nebulizer? I guessed not, but I was hoping otherwise.

After my weekly allergy shots, I had a thorough examination and a test on a respiratory machine. Doctor Luzier was pleased with my continued progress. As we chatted about the old days when I was an asthmatic mess, I slipped in the question I was dying to ask.

"Do you foresee the day when I can be weaned from my machine entirely?"

He shook his head. "You were one of my more serious cases, Arlette. You should be grateful for the nebulizer because it's my opinion that it has saved your life many times."

Dr. Luzier went on to say that I should get the thought of discarding the nebulizer out of my head. I was disappointed but not surprised at his answer because every four to six hours I would commence wheezing and knew it was time to ride that horse again.

After this discussion I did not tell him of my plan to try to carry a baby. Fearing he would say "no," I just didn't ask him. I would go to the Mayo Clinic and maybe I would mention it to the doctor there. Also, I didn't want to lie to Danny. When Danny asked how the checkup went, I could honestly tell him it went great. Then, when he asked what Doctor Luzier said about a pregnancy, I honestly answered that he wasn't at all concerned! Danny was relieved and happy. And so the odyssey began.

Chapter 14

The Trip to Mayo

Kevin didn't take time from work for this first appointment because he knew he wanted to save his vacation days for the actual procedure. We felt like the three Musketeers as we embarked on another medical journey. Ann Murray's voice blasted from the speakers as Christa took her customary place behind the wheel so she and I could sing in the front seat, while her Dad and our Cocker Spaniel, Special, rode in the back.

It was a lovely June day and we were all anxious about the appointments ahead.

Danny's check-up took three outpatient days. He learned nothing new and Danny was told to keep doing as Dr. Janusz advised. We were relieved that they didn't detect any cysts or tumors, but we were hoping that the Mayo Clinic would have the magic cure, or at least something new for this discouraging disease.

Dr. Ory seemed pleased to see Christa again. He detailed a bit of the *in vitro* procedure for us and then explained he would present our case to the board at the Mayo Clinic. We were confident that the unusual circumstances of Mother and Daughter would actually minimize the legal and ethical concerns. But Dr. Ory cautioned us that the board might turn us down. Even so, we felt he was almost as excited as we were. We were grateful to have found him and celebrated this on the trip back to Sioux City.

That night in the motel Christa called Kevin to give him an update. Then she called Curtis and Gina. Christa told her brother that the Doctor said the only drawback he could see was that Mom might think the baby would be hers. Curtis replied, "What the heck, Christa. She thinks our kids are hers!" We all had a good laugh, but Curtis was right. Lucas, Clay and Cole are our children, our GrandCHILDREN. There was no way I could love any baby more then I loved our grandboys.

That Sunday, we went to church in the Catholic Church in Sioux City, as was our custom when we were there. When it was time to go to communion, we were led up the side aisle to receive the host and drink from the cup. As I was going up the aisle, I felt that the statue of Mary was looking at me with eyes that were alive. Her presence was overwhelming as she looked into my eyes. I was nearly overcome with emotion as I felt tears of peace and joy. It was a profound and sacred moment in my life, and I never said a word about it to anyone. I felt that talking about it would diminish the significance. I felt sure that Mary was giving me a sign of her good will and that all would work out as we hoped.

Some months later on a trip to Rapid City, Christa joined us to go visit her brother and family. As we were traveling along we were discussing how this entire project was in God's hands.

Suddenly Christa asked, "Do you remember that time after our trip to the Mayo Clinic when we all attended church in Sioux City?"

"Yes," I answered

"Well," she continued, "when we went up for communion I saw the statue of the Blessed Virgin..."

All at once we were both babbling about our like experience with the statue of the Virgin Mother. It sent chills through us as we realized we had both felt Mary's strong presence and the sense of peace and joy. This was a heartfelt revelation and we were humbled.

Our entire family had been saying *Saint Jude's Prayer,* asking for his intervention so Christa and Kevin could have a child. After our beautiful experience, we fervently turned to Saint Mary as well. Each week I made a vigil to the church where I would spend some quiet time with her and I always lit a candle for the baby-to-be. Mary was a guiding force throughout the entire episode.

Several weeks after our trip to Rochester, Christa received distressing news from Doctor Ory. He called to say the board of the Mayo Clinic had turned down the request for us to begin the *in vitro* procedure. They were unwilling to get involved in the possible legal consequences this could cause.

Christa was crestfallen. She called us with the news and I could tell her heart was nearly broken. Doctor Ory felt so bad for her that he offered to try to locate another doctor for us. Feigning confidence, I told her I was sure he would find someone else, but deep down I was worried. The Mayo Clinic was only three hundred miles for each of us. I knew there were clinics in other states, but could we afford to make trips to them? How often would we need to go? Would there be weeks at a time that we would need to be available, thus necessitating staying in hotels? All of these unanswered questions loomed in my mind, yet I also knew we would forge ahead.

The next few weeks were frustrating. I collected as much information as I could on the clinics that had an *in vitro fertilization* (IVF) program. The statistics I collected were grim. The success rates at that time varied from fourteen to twenty-one percent and the costs were several thousand dollars *per attempt*. I was better off when I was blissfully ignorant of the cost and the odds.

During this time, Christa was trying to contact lawyers and psychologists who dealt exclusively with unusual IVF procedures. Her phone bills were soaring, but she was getting little or no help from those she contacted. Finally, we decided we were not going to worry about that aspect of the problem. We knew we didn't need a psychologist to tell us we were straight with this. We also knew this was about helping family and not about legal contracts. If our plan worked I would simply be an incubator for Christa and Kevin's baby. I would never try to keep their child, and they would never change their minds and not want the baby. Not once did we ever consider such foolish things.

Our hopes soared again in late July when Doctor Ory called Christa. He gave her the name of a doctor at the University of Minnesota Hospital in Minneapolis. Doctor William Phipps was a friend of Doctor Ory's, and Doctor Ory had already told him of our plight. We were ecstatic. We had a name, and the University of Minnesota was exactly three hundred miles from each of us.

Christa contacted Doctor Phipps's office and the earliest we could see him was November 1. When we had seen Doctor Ory in June, it was because we were hoping to have the IVF procedure performed over the summer. Then I would be able to carry a baby during the school months, thus missing very little work. Now we were going to be way off schedule, and this was a PLANNED baby! Still, we were all grateful to have an actual date. The ball was beginning to roll.

On Halloween evening, Danny and I drove to Minneapolis and checked into a Hotel. We wanted to be ready for our appointment bright and early the next morning. Our only snag was that I realized I had forgotten a piece of the nebulizer equipment needed for my breathing treatments. Fortunately, I didn't experience any asthma-related problems during the trip, and had very few breathing problems later, for that matter. Christa and Kevin left Sioux City early on the morning of the November 1, and planned to meet us at the clinic.

We arrived at the clinic just minutes before Christa and Kevin. They were tired, but too exhilarated to be sleepy. My thoughts were racing. I remember thinking, "This is it. We are really here. We are really going to do this." It was almost like a dream. I imagined that it must be something like how astronauts feel when strapped into their seats waiting for their first space adventure. After all the planning, and all the years of hoping, a crucial moment had arrived.

Chapter 15

Doctor Phipps

Christa and Kevin were both called back to an exam room. Then the nurse asked for me also. The nurse was Salina Blatz and she was Dr. Phipps' primary assistant. We didn't know it then, but she would become a dear friend. Her bright smiling face put us at ease.

We were barely seated before Doctor Phipps arrived. Physically, Doctor Phipps was tall, lean and in his thirties. He seemed very matter-of-fact. After brief introductions, he was eager to get down to business.

Dr. Phipps gave us an overview of the IVF procedure, and talked about the odds of a multiple birth. His precise and professional manner contrasted with Christa and me. Everything he said sounded so positive to us that we could hardly contain ourselves. We held hands and absorbed every word. Finally, Doctor Phipps stopped talking about medical procedure. He leaned back and honored us with the most engaging smile, and at that moment a different side of his personality shone through.

When Christa exclaimed that twins or even triplets would be great as far as she was concernd, Dr. Phipps grinned and said, "Christa, be nice to your mother." The ice was broken, and we knew we liked him and felt he liked us too.

Next, he needed to examine Christa. Kevin and I stayed in the room with her while Dr. Phipps did a routine exam. While performing the exam, he explained the egg retrieval procedure in more detail. We all wanted Danny to hear this, so Christa sent Kevin out to the waiting room to get him. Kevin, ever the practical joker, told Dan to hurry back because they needed to draw a blood sample from him. Danny kept asking, "Me? Why would they need to take blood from me?" We all got a good chuckle from this as Danny realized he had been "Uchytized" by Kevin.

Doctor Phipps discreetly continued to examine Christa to determine how healthy her ovaries were and decide if the eggs would be retrieved laparoscopically or vaginally. Casually, Doctor Phipps mentioned that even though Christa was born with Mayer-Rokitansky-Kuster-Hauser Syndrome, medically she was absolutely perfect except for lacking a uterus. Christa blushed, Kevin beamed and Danny and I were just plain happy.

After Christa's exam, it was my turn. Danny and Kevin went back to the waiting room as I undressed and got into a gown. The procedure started out routinely enough, and Doctor was saying positive things about my "proven uterus." Christa and I smiled at one another feeling very confident. Suddenly a puzzled look came over his face as he looked at the ultrasound screen. Immediately I asked him what was wrong. He could see what appeared to be a large cyst or tumor on one of my ovaries. This would have to be examined more closely before we could begin the *in vitro* procedure.

Dr. Phipps could see we were alarmed. He reassured both Christa and me that he was confident it was just a benign cyst, but he could not in good conscience proceed until I had a clean bill of health. This was an unexpected delay. Doctor Phipps explained that I would have to go back to Aberdeen, have another ultrasound done by my gynecologist. I would probably be on pills for one month, then I would have to have another ultrasound. If the mass did not shrink in this time, I would need to have surgery to have it removed and biopsied.

We also talked about my asthma, which seemed to have improved in recent weeks. Then, I tentatively broached the subject that concerned me most. It was apparent that I was starting menopause and I was worried this would make things more difficult or even impossible. Much to my relief, Doctor Phipps assured me that this played no part at all. In fact, he explained they were going to squelch my ovarian function and try to synchronize Christa's cycles with my cycles.

Christa had been taking her temperature and keeping a chart to determine the time of the month when she ovulated. Because of the unexpected delay, she would need to continue this procedure until our next visit to the University. During this time, she and Kevin could not heat their waterbed as that might interfere with getting an accurate temperature. Christa had been dutifully checking her temperature seven days a week and she would continue. We were determined to do everything exactly as we were instructed. Even if that meant Christa and Kevin would sleep on an unheated mattress in the cold winter months of November and December. I was glad that wasn't me!

While I got dressed, Doctor Phipps talked to Kevin and Christa, asking medical questions and getting health background information. Then all three of us had to have blood drawn to test for AIDS, Rubella and various other diseases. Even though Danny and I had been monogamous for twenty-six years, I was anxious to have an AIDS test because he'd had that blood transfusion in 1989. That fact had always haunted me, and now I was eager for the results to come back.

The four of us waited in an examining room for the test results while we received more instructions about what would be involved when the problem with my ovary was resolved. Doctor Phipps wanted to get as much of the preliminary work out of the way because he realized this trip was time-consuming and expensive.

His nurse, Salina, was telling us what we would have to do to prepare ourselves physically for the actual retrieval and transfer. She brought in a kit and explained that each day for two weeks an injection of Lupron would have to be self-administered in the upper leg. Thinking she meant only Christa, I assured my surprised-looking daughter that she could do it. After all, look how diabetic children learn to give themselves insulin shots. When the nurse quickly explained that I, too, would be doing this, I was shocked. Me, give myself an injection? My stomach turned over. I was sure God had let me have asthma instead of diabetes because I wasn't the type who was able to do this.

When the nurse was done explaining the procedure, Christa and I had to practice on ourselves. We were nervous, but as our husbands looked on with cat-like grins, we both finally made the plunge.

It wasn't that bad. I was expecting it to be much harder and more painful. On my second attempt, I hesitated at the last minute and that time it hurt. Christa laughed at me because I was talking so bravely, but my actions reflected how I really felt. Danny and Kevin were thoroughly enjoying this and tried to keep our spirits up with good-natured ribbing. We felt almost giddy with excitement.

Christa then asked the critical question, "How much does this procedure cost?"

"The cost is seven thousand dollars for each IVF attempt," Salina explained.

That wiped the smiles off our faces. We knew Christa and Kevin's insurance would not cover even one IVF attempt. We were also told that the money had to be paid up front and the cost was the same whether or not the procedure was successful. We were aware that this was an expensive procedure but it was still a sobering reality.

The last thing on the agenda that day was to meet with the clinic psychologist. This was a very brief appointment consisting of an introduction and a homework assignment. We were given a six-page test to be complete and mail back to her.

We had been at the clinic the entire day. We were all starving and decided to find a nice restaurant before heading back to our respective homes. At the restaurant we toasted the future which looked brighter then ever. We were all certain my problem was just a minor delay and nothing more. Christa and Kevin would borrow the "baby money," as they called it, from the bank. We all loved Doctor Phipps and Salina and our hopes were high. We were definitely on our way!

Chapter 16

The Delay

Back in Aberdeen, I made a November 15 appointment to see my gynecologist. Dr. Hovland made an ultrasound examination of the mass and, as predicted, put me on birth control pills to see if the alien thing on my ovary would shrink. In December the tests revealed the mass was the same size. The doctor determined that he would have to look at it through a laparoscope. This minor, same-day procedure was set for mid-December.

Danny accompanied me to the hospital that morning at six-thirty. I told Doctor Hovland that no matter what they found they must leave my uterus intact. That morning, I reiterated this wish to the nurse who was prepping me for surgery. I was concerned enough that I insisted that my wishes be put in writing. Even if cancer was found, my uterus could not be tampered with or removed during this procedure. I feared waking up and hearing that my ovaries were cancerous and while they were removing them they felt it would be in my best interest to remove my uterus, too. I considered my uterus a vital organ and wanted it left in my body.

Fortunately, the mass proved to be comprised of benign cysts. Doctor Hovland aspirated the largest one and drained one or two more. I was home in bed by mid-afternoon.

We called Christa immediately to give her the good news. Now we could make another appointment at the University. The roadblocks were being eliminated and we were on our way once again. While I was attending to my physical matters, Christa and Kevin were working on the financial details. While Kevin was at work one day, an eager Christa had gone to the bank and been turned down for the loan. Obviously, a baby could not be collateral for a bank. This wasn't a car loan. In tears, she shared this information with Kevin. He comforted her and assured her that he would go to the bank and use their vehicles for collateral. He promised her that he would have the money when we went back to the University. Kevin and the bank came through.

It was shortly after this when several of my colleagues and friends asked me why I was making trips to the University of Minnesota. Evasively, I told those who asked that I was going for check-ups. This didn't satisfy anyone – especially since the reason someone travels from Aberdeen to University of Minnesota is usually for a very serious illness. They were concerned, especially given my history of respiratory problems. Ironically, my asthma had actually improved and I no longer needed my nebulizer. However, we hadn't planned to tell anyone outside the family about what we were trying to do.

One day as I ate lunch, I realized it was unfair to make my friends worry about my health when I was fine. As I looked around the room, I felt they deserved to know the real reason for my trips to Minnesota.

"I'm trying to get pregnant!" I stated to everyone's shock. Then I quickly went on to explain what we were hoping to do. Everyone in the teacher's lounge perked up and all seemed genuinely interested and supportive. After I left the lounge, a few people commented that they thought I was crazy.

The really unsettling aspect of sharing this information with others was I felt like I was invading Christa's privacy. In all these years we had shared the information about Christa's syndrome with very few people. Now it seemed peculiar to tell something we had kept private for so long. I called Christa when I got home and she said she understood and that it was fine with her. She added that she hoped everyone would need to know soon!

A couple of weeks after that conversation our local newspaper called and wanted to know if they could do a feature about me and our newest family-member to be. At first, I was so surprised I couldn't follow the conversation or understand what they wanted. After I recovered from my amazement, I declined the interview. I tried to explain that there really was no news, we were just trying to have a baby for Christa and Kevin.

The reporter was very nice and asked, "Could I check with you now and then to see if there is any news?"

"We never even entertained the thought of going public," I told her.

We chatted more and I assured her that if we ever decided to go public with our story, I would call her.

That evening Danny and I talked about the call.

"You know, if things work out it might not be a bad idea to talk to our local paper," Danny suggested. "That way our entire community would know at one time and we wouldn't have to explain what we are doing to acquaintances."

After a brief discussion we basically tabled the idea. We had real hurdles to jump before dealing with the media or telling community members would even have to be considered.

My nightly prayers included the Saint Jude's prayer. Each night I petitioned for Danny's health, Curtis' hopes, and Christa's and Kevin's dreams. As we moved forward, I knew Curtis, Gina, and the boys, as well as many other family members were praying for this miracle, too. My library assistant and dear friend, Pam McLaughlin, offered solid support on a daily basis. I was aware of and thankful for her prayers. She is the kind of person who seems to have a direct link to the Almighty because her faith is such a part of who she is.

Christmas of 1990 was delightful. We celebrated with our children and grandsons. It was exciting to watch Curtis and Gina enjoy their own children. You could see the love and happiness in their eyes as the boys opened presents, celebrated Mass and went to bed anticipating Santa's gifts in the morning. Maybe, just maybe, Christa would get her chance, too.

Christa made our next appointment at the University of Minnesota for January 28. It was not possible for either Danny or Kevin to go, and it wasn't really necessary. So, for the first time, just us two women embarked on the journey to Minneapolis. I left Aberdeen and Christa left Sioux City about the same time early in the morning. We were meeting in Brookings, South Dakota, a drive of about one hundred fifty miles for each of us. After meeting we would travel into Minneapolis for the appointment.

The last eighty or ninety miles to Minneapolis were treacherous. The roads were snow-packed and slippery. Consequently, we were late for our two o'clock appointment. This worried us, but Doctor Phipps was very understanding. Everything went great during this check up. After what seemed like my hundredth ultrasound, I was declared fit! Then Doctor Phipps examined Christa to see how her ovaries were doing. We had a blood test to determine our ovulation cycles, and were happy to hear we were nearly in sync with one another.

It was time to get the instructions for Phase Two. Doctor Phipps explained showed me the Estrogen patches I would need to wear and explained the charts used to keep track of them. This seemed very complicated and he patiently repeated until he was certain I understood. I would need to wear my first patch on February 8. Next, he again explained the injection regimen. Mine would be easy. For the next two weeks I would have to give myself one injection in the upper thigh. Christa needed to give herself an injection in the thigh. She also needed another daily injection that involved complicated mixing. This shot had to be administered in her buttocks. Fortunately, a nurse was always on duty where Christa worked and she could enlist help with the more difficult shots.

Doctor Phipps was very detailed in his instructions and we understood how important it was to do everything exactly as directed. The seriousness couldn't dampen our enthusiasm. With each positive tidbit we heard, Christa and I would bubble. I'm not sure what Doctor Phipps thought of us, but we looked on him as as our luminary. He radiated quiet confidence, and personified hope. When he would deviate from the seriousness of our mission and permit a smile, he lit up the room. We sincerely loved him for what he was trying to do for us.

The last instructions of the day were for Christa. She was to travel to Sioux Falls, South Dakota, the following week for another ultrasound to see how her oocytes were coming. This would be closer to her home community than the University. The physician in Sioux Falls would call Doctor Phipps with the results.

After two progesterone shots in my buttocks, we made a stop at the university pharmacy to get our prescriptions. Then we were our way back to Brookings, South Dakota, to spend the night. The Lupron prescription cost nearly nine hundred dollars. The other medicines, Metrodin and Perganol, cost an additional two hundred dollars. This was a lot of money for us, but people spend thousands of dollars buying a vehicle. If Christa and Kevin got a child from this, no price would be too high.

We arrived in Brookings, physically tired but emotionally exhilarated. Christa and I both needed to give ourselves shots that night. Practice was over and now it was the real thing. We couldn't mess up or chicken out. We were so professional as we filled the syringes and tapped out the air bubbles, but the nervous giggles started as we geared up for the plunge. We couldn't help but laugh at how silly we looked. We felt like explorers embarking on a journey, a journey that could end in tragic heartbreak or discovery of the real world of parenthood!

I needed to be back in Aberdeen by noon the following day for meetings at the school. After a nice breakfast and a warm hug, Christa and I headed in opposite directions.

The drive home provided me with thoughtful silence, and my thoughts were about Christa and what she must be going through. She was literally putting all her eggs in one basket. Financially, emotionally, physically, and mentally; this was a one shot chance. The trips, the cost – if this didn't work, all our hopes would be dashed. Maybe we could try a second time, but one had to be realistic. How deep in debt could Christa and Kevin go? The emotional roller coaster would also take its toll. I knew it was now or never.

I prayed a lot on my drive home that day. *Dear God, let your grace shine upon us. Christa will be such a good mother. Look how she loves her nephews, Lucas, Clay and Cole. She's only twenty-two and yet she handles her role as stepmom to Justin with such patience and love. Please God, please God, please God...*

That evening I felt so important and brave as I took out my Lupron kit. Danny was duly impressed as I prepared the needle and boldly stuck myself. Words could not express how I appreciated his support and alliance in this small step toward a very big dream. Reality started to sink in. We were actually working toward a baby for Christa and Kevin. I vowed to eat right, gets lots of rest, drink plenty of water and try not to be too stressed.

Curtis, Gina, Lucas, Clay and Cole came for a visit the next weekend as did Christa and Kevin. The boys sat around the dining room table and colored while the adults visited. Curtis mentioned something about me getting pregnant and six-year-old Lucas piped up, "Gramma, are YOU going to have a baby?"

We all looked at one another. Then I explained that Christa and Kevin were hoping to have a baby. I went on to tell him that Christa was born without a uterus.

"A uterus is where a baby grows and lives until it is ready to be born," I explained simply. "It's like a heart or a lung. Christa doesn't have a uterus of her own, so she and Kevin are using mine until their baby is ready to be born."

"Oh, okay," he said as he resumed coloring.

That was easy and it never did become difficult or clouded for any of the grandchildren. They all understood the basic concept and they did not have any problems with it. Later, in a *Time Magazine* interview I described it in these terms. "Instead of the birds and the bees, there are the birds and bees and butterflies, too."

Chapter 17

The Big Time Arrives

Christa received a call from Doctor Phipps on February 12, 1991. He told her she needed to take her shot of Metrodin right then. It was 9:30 in the morning and luckily there was a nurse present to do the deed. Doctor Phipps also informed her that she would need to have her Pergonal shot at 4:30 that afternoon and to be as precise as possible. Christa would need to have the Metrodin for two days and a daily Pergonal shot (a combination of hormones to stimulate follicle development in the ovaries) shot for the next eight days. Christa called to tell us this great news. Everything was moving quickly and smoothly.

On February 15, Doctor Phipps called. He directed me to have blood drawn at the clinic for an estradiol check. Estradiol is one of the estrogens produced naturally by the ovaries. It is also important in preparing the uterus for, and making it receptive to, implantation by an embryo. Dr. Phipps said he would check on the estradiol results. That evening he called again.

"Add an extra estradiol patch tonight, Arlette," he instructed. "Label it patch 'A' and keep it on until Sunday. Otherwise, continue the schedule, but be sure to add the patch."

The calls and the instructions reinforced for me just how precisely the procedure had to be followed. It also made me appreciate the individualized care that doctor Phipps gave his patients.

After five days had passed, it was time for Christa and Kevin to go to Minneapolis for an extended stay. The date was February 17, our son Curtis' birthday. We all felt this was a good sign. The exact length of time

Kevin and Christa would need to stay in Minneapolis could not be determined, but would depend on Christa's oocytes. These are the immature eggs and the word is pronounced *oh-oh-sites*. Together with layers of surrounding cells the oocytes form follicles in the ovaries. In adult women, one of the ripening follicles ejects a mature oocyte each month resulting in ovulation. Dr. Phipps was managing this ripening process to promote oocyte development.

Doctor Phipps planned to monitor Christa closely with daily ultrasounds. When the oocytes were ready, they would be removed immediately. When this happened, I would need to get to Minneapolis. We all assumed this would take place the following weekend. Were we wrong!

Two days later, on Tuesday, February 19, at about four in the afternoon, Doctor Phipps called me at school. He told me I needed to get to the University of Minnesota Hospital that night. Things were progressing much more rapidly then expected and the retrieval was scheduled for Thursday morning.

My mind reeled as I tried to reach Danny. He was working out of town. I had his itinerary and started calling his customers, asking them to have my husband call me. Fortunately, Danny got one of the messages and called me at about five that afternoon.

We discussed whether or not I should drive to Minneapolis, but finally decided I should just fly. Danny would drive there as soon as possible. This was not an easy decision for me because I do not like to fly. By seven that evening I was on a little prop jet, tightly gripping the arm rests, praying and sweating – and that was before we even left the ground. For me, this simple act ranked high on the sacrifice scale. Only a closed curtain separated the pilots from the passengers. It didn't allay my fear when the flight attendant asked me to move across from the only other passenger so we would better balance the airplane.

"Oh God!" I thought. "Now I really am worried this plane will go down."

After giving the preflight instructions, the attendant didn't even fly with us, but immediately departed. I worried that if the plane did crash, Christa would carry that guilt around with her. Talk about Jewish mothers who worry. Irish/German mothers worry just as much.

One hour later, I arrived safely in Minneapolis. I took an airport shuttle to the hotel and checked into the double room I would share with Christa and Kevin. They had to leave for the hospital. Christa needed an injection of gonadotropins at midnight. This combination of hormones replicates those the body secretes to encourage follicle or egg development and stimulate ovulation. This would be her last injection before the retrieval procedure. Her back end had been stuck from two-to-five times every day for the last several weeks. One more thing over. It was like a count down.

On Wednesday, Christa and I went to the hospital for our final ultrasound exams. We both got good reports. My uterus looked good and Christa's eggs did also. We had the rest of the day off.

The three of us passed the time playing the game *Jenga*. Kevin proved to be quite good at this, employing strategy and demonstrating a competitive streak. Christa and I were both gleeful when he would topple the blocks on his turn. We had a fun day, and I was grateful for this time. It was a wonderful opportunity to develop a closer relationship with my son-in-law. He is, by nature, a private person and this extra time together was a gift.

Early the following morning, the three of us arrived at the hospital. Eager yet anxious, we waited for Danny. He had been putting in long hours at work in hopes of being able to be with us at the retrieval. We earnestly prayed he would arrive before Christa went into the retrieval room.

After Christa was gowned and in her hospital bed, a nurse inserted an IV into Christa's arm. This was for the morphine drip she would receive in the operating room. Time crawled, but no Danny. The two hours we waited seemed much longer without him. The three of us played twenty questions and tried to occupy our minds.

Finally, Salina came and it was such a relief to see her and listen to her explain the procedure in detail. At 9:30, Christa was wheeled into the operating room with Kevin at her side. In a surgical cap and gown, I was also allowed to observe the retrieval.

They started the morphine drip and warned Christa the procedure would be quite painful, but tolerable. A very long needle, probably ten inches in length, was inserted vaginally. Then it was poked into an ovary. The procedure is so unpleasant because the tough ovarian wall has to be punctured with each attempt. Christa was in extreme pain, but no sound came out of her mouth. Only the tears running from the corners of her eyes indicated what she felt.

"Christa, don't ever let anyone tell you that you didn't have labor," I assured her, "because you're having your labor!"

Each follicle retrieval attempt meant another prick into an ovary and targeting the ovaries was not easy. It was like trying to stick a needle into a balloon floating in the air. The ovary would move away making penetration a challenge. After each puncture Salina would go out with the needle and come back to report the success. The pain Christa endured was worth it when Salina reported "Two eggs in that one" or "One on that try" and so on.

We were also watching this spellbinding sight on an ultrasound monitor. "Watch," I would encourage Christa, hoping to take her mind off the pain. She and Kevin held tight to one another as time and time again the needle was inserted.

Finally, the needle was too dull to retrieve any more follicles. Doctor Phipps saw one more egg he felt he should retrieve. Christa finally spoke and said, "Oh no!"

As much as my heart ached for her, I tried to be positive as I told her, "Just think, Christa, this might be the very one. This might be your baby. Hang on."

After nearly fifty minutes, it was finally over. Doctor Phipps had retrieved eleven eggs and Doctor Hensleigh was busy taking care of them. Christa was wheeled back to her room to recover.

Kevin and I felt so sorry for her. I have never seen anyone more nauseous. If she moved or tried to lift her head she would be sick. This was an aftereffect of the morphine and continued until late afternoon. When Christa could tolerate sitting in a wheelchair, we got her ready to go to the car. While Kevin was pulling the car to the curb, Christa was certain she was going to be sick right there in the lobby. Eventually, we made it back to the motel where she rested for several more hours. Her suffering was as severe as any birth pain.

That evening Danny arrived with our dog, Special. By then, Christa felt better and was eager to share details of the day's excitement. The rest of the evening occupied ourselves by playing a French card game called Milborn and drinking grapefruit juice mixed with 7-Up. We were all in a celebratory mood and made toasts with our concoction.

Christa called Curtis and Gina, and Kevin called his parents. Of course, this added to the festivity. My sister, Darlene, then called from Phoenix and my brother, Cliff, from Rapid City. They were passing on the information to the other relatives. Everyone was eager to hear how things were going. The next morning the telephone woke us. Doctor Hensleigh, the embryologist or "Egg Doctor," wanted to speak with

Christa. We were sharing a double room to cut down on costs, so we could overhear Christa as she spoke with the Doctor Hensleigh. The eggs had been analyzed, incubated and then fertilized with Kevin's sperm. Of the eleven eggs, four were viable. This meant fertilization had occurred resulting in four of the eggs. This was excellent news and we were all very pleased. Things were progressing nicely.

Friday was a relatively free day. My progesterone injection was the only scheduled appointment that day. It took only a few moments. I would need one of these injections each day, possibly through the first trimester of the pregnancy. Among other things, progesterone plays a role in halting the monthly menstrual cycle and making the uterus hospitable to maintaining pregnancy. Ironically, progesterone-like substances are also a key part of the contraceptive effects of birth control pills.

I watched closely as the nurse prepared the shot, then I had her explain exactly how to give the injection. I realized I would need to do this myself. Every day meant weekends too, and I didn't know anyone who would want to do that. This was going to be more difficult than the Lupron. That little needle seemed insignificant compared to the four inch spike this required.

Progesterone is a thick oil that requires a large needle, and it takes strong thumbs to push the oil out of the syringe. Another snag was the injection site. This had to be in the gluteus medius, muscle on the backside of the hip area. I could choose between the right or left side, but I needed to stay within an area that was only about the size of an orange. I hoped I could manage.

To maintain a sense of normalcy, we spent the rest of Friday sight-seeing. We visited a beautiful arboretum. Then, Danny and Kevin wanted to investigate some of the area grocery stores. I wanted to see the famed Theater In The Round, but the two people who spend some of each day in a grocery store wanted to visit grocery stores! Christa agreed with them, so off we went. We compared cookie and cracker sections, critiqued displays, made notes on the size of the different departments, among other exciting activities.

That evening we entertained ourselves and tried to stay calm. We played *Jenga* again. The challenge of the game is to stack blocks into a tall tower, then pull out lower blocks without toppling the tower. We were counting down until Saturday morning when the four fertilized embryos were to be transferred into my uterus. This week had been a long time in coming. Now that it was here, the whole thing seemed unreal. Everything was going so smoothly. All of the puzzle pieces were falling into place and we prayed for success. Life, at least my life, had always involved a complication or two. Perhaps we had exhausted those complications with what Christa had already endured. Now we were relying on medical precision to overcome obstacles, but I'm sure our prayers also helped. We prayed even more intensely for God's blessing even as we headed into the next phase of our odyssey.

On Saturday morning, we arrived at the hospital at about nine o'clock. The first thing on the agenda was my progesterone shot. After a few more instructions to bolster my confidence, I gave myself the injection. I'd be lying if I said it was easy. It was painful, and I had a terrible time pushing the oil into my muscle. The awkward position didn't help, but finally the mission was accomplished. Danny felt sorry for me and wanted to help, but he didn't think he could stick that needle into me. Finally, we decided I would draw the oil into the syringe and stick the needle into my hip. Danny would depress the plunger to deliver the injection, and then remove the needle. This was going to be interesting.

Before Doctor Phipps arrived, Doctor Hensleigh stuck his head into my room and asked us if we wanted to look at the fertilized eggs. This was an unexpected surprise. He led us to a small room where we were instructed to just stand in the doorway and watch the television monitor on the wall. In a matter of seconds we were viewing Christa and Kevin's fertilized eggs. You could count the cells. It was an awesome sight, looking at a miracle in progress!

We all were overcome with emotion. Kevin and Christa had their arms around one another. Danny slipped his arm around me and whispered in awe, "We are looking at our potential grandchildren."

We have an actual photograph of what we viewed on the screen and I plan to have it enlarged and put on the wall with all the family pictures. It is Chelsea and Chad's first photo.

Salina and Doctor Phipps arrived and before any official work began we took some photos of them and Doctor Hensleigh. These photos show a warm and caring trio and that's exactly what they were. Doctor Phipps explained that he would transfer all four embryos, in hopes of one grabbing hold.

"A woman's eggs fertilize much more frequently than most people realize," he explained. "Whether that fertilized egg actually attaches to the lining of the uterus and goes on to develop is another matter. Many times, as often as seventy percent, there is no attachment. When that happens, they are simply absorbed back into the body."

We were all hoping at least one of these four would attach. Doctor Phipps went on to remind us that there was a chance that two, three or even all four of the eggs would attach.

You might be wondering if, as Catholics, our decision to proceed with IVF resulted in conflict with the Church. At the time, we were unaware of the Church's position. Since there had never been a case like ours in the United States, we were breaking new ground. In addition, none of us considered what we were doing to be a surrogate situation. Usually, a surrogate is someone who is hired to provide a service and there is an exchange of money. We later learned that the official Church docinte had been enunciated in a 1987 document entitled *Instruction on Respect for Human Life in Its Origin and on the Dignity of Procreation*. The teaching maintains that procreation should only be the result of intercourse within the marital relationship, and the Church is strictly opposed to the use of third-party (heterologous) donation of sperm or eggs to produce embryos.

The Church is also sensitive to the pain of infertile couples, as well as being concerned with the moral, spiritual and ethical considerations associated with scientifically-assisted procreation. There has been significant discussion among pastors (both Catholic and Protestant) about the use of a couple's own sperm and egg to achieve pregnancy through IVF procedures. While the Church is officially opposed to IVF, we learned that a number of Catholic pastors feel that the use of medical science to help a loving, married couple have their own biological child should be viewed as an appropriate reproductive choice.

Chicago's late Cardinal Joseph L. Bernardin, in an address at the University of Chicago in 1987, said, "I have heard the pain of loving couples, Catholic and non-Catholic, who desperately want the gift of a child. My heart reaches out to them. Theirs is a difficult burden, and I share their pain. We must offer them love, support and understanding. And in the end, after careful and conscientious reflection on this teaching, they must make their own decision."

At the time, however, we were unaware of specific Church policy addressing our unique circumstances. We agreed completely with the Church's teachings about the sanctity of marriage and life. Doctor Phipps understood that no matter how many embryos developed, it was in God's hands. We would not even consider aborting one or more fetuses. We were praying for a baby, and one healthy baby would make us happy. If we were blessed with more, they would be God's gift.

Doctor Phipps informed Danny and me that for the two weeks following the transfer, we would have to refrain from sexual intercourse. There were laughs all around because Doctor Phipps had told us on a previous trip that we would need to refrain from sex for the two weeks prior to implantation also. After some embarrassed looks and red faces, Danny exclaimed, "I didn't know I'd have to sacrifice too!"

That broke the tension. Kevin even joined in giving Danny some good-natured teasing. The four of us had shared so much. After the initial shock of discussing our sex life in front of our children, this too became just another part of the medical procedure. Little did we know what two weeks here and two weeks there would turn into.

Now it was my turn to go to the operating room. Christa accompanied me for the few minutes needed to make the transfer. This was done in the *lithotomy* position, the same as for a pelvic exam. The procedure was virtually painless and took just a few minutes. With the implantation procedure completed, the final phase of the *in vitro fertilization* was now in progress.

For the next four hours I had to remain on my back with my head lower than my hips. Danny, Christa and Kevin offered to stay with me, but I told them I preferred solitude.

I did not want to talk, or cough, or move for the next four hours. We had come this far and trying to chitchat for four hours was not what I needed to do. I wanted to concentrate all my energy on a positive outcome. I had a cassette tape of waves and other ocean sounds, my rosary, and a tape of Anne Murray. She had been with us on all our other trips and it was soothing to listen to her familiar voice.

The first two hours went by rather quickly. I did a lot of praying and felt very peaceful. Then a rather uncomfortable bodily function started to interfere with the serenity. I needed to go to the bathroom ... bad! I was just sick about this.

The nurse answered my call light and when I told her my dilemma she assured me this was very normal. Often, the bladder is touched during the procedure and this contributes to the sense of urgency. She continued to tell me that many others have had to empty their bladders. When I asked if she knew about the pregnancy success rates among those women who emptied their bladders versus those who did not in similar circumstances, she looked at me like I was demented. I sent her away without emptying my bladder and she said I should call again, "If I needed her."

Unfortunately, a short time later I desperately needed her. There was no way I could hold out for another hour or more. The nurse brought me a bed pan and helped to elevate my hips just enough to accommodate the pan. The physical relief, however, brought with it a lot of emotional turmoil.

My tranquility was also broken by the cries and screams of a woman in the next room who was in the throes of labor. I wasn't concerned about what was in store for me, and I never did cry or scream during labor or birth. I felt sorry that she was in such agony. I wonder why some women have so much more difficulty and if it is related to the amount of time spent in labor. The longest labor I ever experienced was with Curtis and that was only about four hours.

I hoped the woman next door would deliver her baby soon. I also thought it ironic that while "we" were trying to get pregnant, a woman was trying to give birth. This was, of course, a hospital and we were on the maternity, floor but I had never realized that until the reality of this poor woman's labor pierced the tranquility. When Christa and the guys came back a short time later, I immediately told her about my potty break. Christa was sure it wouldn't affect our chances. I hoped she was right.

The nurse came in to tell me I could get up and dress to leave. I had some trepidation about going vertical. It seemed that if I stood up, everything would fall out. Yet, I knew I couldn't lie there for the next nine months. I got out of the bed and Christa helped me dress. Then we just walked out. It seemed so strange, but we were done.

The four of us went back to the hotel. I laid on the bed while we quietly visited. No shouts, no toasts, just a suspension in time. Everything that could be said, had been. It was a time for quiet contemplation.

Christa and Kevin had been in Minneapolis for a week and they decided to start for home. Danny and I stayed one more night so I could remain supine for the next twenty-four hours. We said our good byes and my hug and kiss from Kevin and Christa was extra special.

"Ten more days of waiting," Christa whispered, "just ten more days and then we will know."

Danny and I both dozed the afternoon away. Later he brought food to the room. After an evening of television it was time to sleep once again. Danny and I held hands as we prayed together for our children, our grandchildren and a miracle.

We checked out of the Holiday Inn on Sunday morning, February 24. After fueling the car, we stopped at a fast food place for a quick breakfast. I ordered orange juice and a muffin. This was as nutritious as I could get with takeout food. When we got home I was determined to eat only healthy foods, but for now I didn't want to get in and out of the car any more than I had to. Special, who is used to riding on my lap in the car, was banished to the back seat where he felt sorry for himself. He was not neglected on the trip but he couldn't understand why I did not want him on my tummy.

As we drove home, Danny and I visited like we always did. My mind wandered to Christa and Kevin, imagining how stressful the next ten days would be for them. Silently I prayed for this to work. This was one of thousands of prayers in our vigil. Silent little messages to God, to the Saints, and of course to Mother Mary. As we visited, and when we were quiet, these prayers were continually being thought. Sometimes it was just a "please God," but in our hearts there was a continuous request that God would bless us with the gift of grandchildren.

Chapter 18

The Good News

On Monday morning, Danny and I prepared for work as always. The only variation in our routine was my daily progesterone injection. Our first team attempt worked reasonably well. On the count of three I stabbed the needle in. Danny was surprised at how much strength it took to squeeze the oil from the syringe. The only real hitch was when he removed the needle at an upward angle instead of pulling it straight out. There was a slight "tongggg." Some pain, a little blood, not bad.

With time, this enterprise evolved into a comedy routine. Danny, forever making jokes, would come at me with the needle like he was going to jab me. Often this was accompanied by diabolical laughter. Many mornings he would leap out of bed exclaiming how this part of the day gave him reason to get up.

Each day I checked and rechecked my estrogen chart. The estrogen regimen included transdermal medication patches that had to be added or removed. This was rather complex and required attention to detail. Sometimes patches had to be added in the morning, sometimes in the evening. The patches were numbered and I had specific instructions such as, "Take off patch two and three; Keep on four, five and six; Add seven, eight, and nine." I never wore more than six patches at a time so the numbers changed to match those I would take off or put on.

I also needed to mark the areas on my abdomen where the patches had been applied and try to rotate the application as much as possible. After the first two weeks I didn't need to make marks any more. They were there showing bright red. They were irritated, itching skin surfaces exactly the size and shape of the patch I had removed.

The estrogen patches stayed on during showers, but I learned to remove those I needed to, then shower, scrubbing that area of irritated skin, before adding the new patches. This was always a relief.

Fortunately, my work at school during this time kept my mind busy during the day. It was good to be back in the routine without planning for a trip. Back in Sioux City, Christa also was happy to be busy all day. Only when things slowed down was there time to ponder and worry about the success or failure of our venture.

Nights gave way for time to think and pray, pray, pray. It got so I would wake from a deep sleep and find myself in the middle of a prayer. It was continual. I would make the sign of the cross as I drove, I prayed as I cooked, and this is when I started my weekly practice of visiting Mary's statue at our church. Who more than Our Holy Mother would understand what a mother's love for her child? Who more than Mary would understand Christa's dream to be a mother?

Mary seemed to already have reached out to us in the church in Sioux City. I felt she understood and I felt drawn to her. My lunches now consisted of healthy tuna sandwiches, vegetables, fruit and of course milk. IF there was a baby growing, he or she was going to be nourished properly. I dutifully drank six to eight glasses of water each day, as well as another four glasses of milk, plus juice. This made it difficult to have room for food but I made sure I was properly nourished.

Each night we talked with Christa and Kevin. The first week went well, but the last three days of the wait were hellish. Christa literally became sick with nerves and I developed a headache that would retreat to the background but not leave. Calls intensified between our three families. Christa and Kevin, Curtis and Gina, and Danny and I were all on edge. Relatives started calling to tell us they were wishing us the best and that we were in their prayers.

Christa's friends at her work were supporting her just like my friends and colleagues were supporting me. We knew we were the beneficiaries of many prayers from many people, and we were grateful.

Finally the day arrived. March 5, 1991. Kevin reluctantly left town that morning for meetings in another city. Poor Christa! This was not the day for him to be gone. Danny also was going to be on the road until six or seven that evening. Poor me!

Kevin, like Danny, had been thinking so positively up until the last day or two. Then he started to worry that we all could be in for a giant letdown. He realized our hopes were so high that we were not emotionally prepared for a negative answer. This was one day he needed to be in two places at once. Whatever the answer, Christa would need him by her side. Yet, none of us could afford to risk our jobs. Regardless, our work ethic would have prevented us from shirking our work responsibilities.

Before school, I went to the clinic hoping they could do the blood test early. "Maybe," I thought, "the results will be back from the lab before Kevin has to leave town."

No luck. The nurse that "does blood" didn't come in before noon. I'm not sure how I got through the morning. Thankfully, students keep a library busy and eventually it was lunch time.

I had an appointment to have my blood drawn over the noon hour. We would get the lab results later in the day. In front of the clinic, I took time to say one more prayer. Then I took a few deep breaths to calm myself and went inside.

The receptionist was a former classmate of Christa's, as well as the daughter of my gynecologist. We visited briefly and then the nurse called me back to draw my blood. This was over and I was back at my desk in a half hour. Now we would wait some more.

The minutes ticked by, one by one by one. It was a relief when the school day ended and I could go home. Many of the staff wished me good luck as I left. Several hugged me. Some tried to take the pressure off by suggesting we could always try again. Pam, my assistant, said her family was praying and I should let her know as soon as possible. I left school knowing that no matter what the lab results were, I wouldn't be the same person when I returned to the school the next day.

The phone was ringing as I walked in our front door. It was Christa wondering if I'd heard anything. She was nearly distraught with worry that we would not hear that day. She suggested I call the doctor's office and make sure they called with the news as soon as they knew the results. I called Christa back to tell her the doctor's office had assured me that they would call with the results as soon as the hospital sent them over. Then I went about gathering all my security blankets and headed for my safe spot. My bed.

My security consisted of my rosary, my portable phone, a prayer card, and the Bible. Our dog, Special, and our cat, Boom Boom, joined me on the bed. They seemed to sense that something important was happening and they wanted to be part of it. Just as the three of us got settled, the doorbell rang. At first, I ignored it. I didn't want to deal with answering the door, talking to someone, or even walking across the room when the call came. It was something I couldn't contemplate. The bell continued to ring, and Special continued to bark. Irritated, I got up and hurried to the entry.

It was my sister, Marlis, and my dear mother. They wondered if I had heard anything. Their interest and concern touched me, but I explained that I needed to be alone for the call. They understood perfectly. Just as we were saying goodbye, the phone rang in my hand. Immediately, I became light-headed. It seemed dreamlike as I started up the foyer steps that led to the living room. I knew instinctively that this was the call, and that I shouldn't be standing when I got the long-awaited news.

My mother was waiting in my sister's car, but Marlis was still in the foyer. She wanted to hear the news, and I wanted her to know. My feet felt like cement as I tried to hurry to a chair, but I was worried the caller would hang up. I was in the middle of my living room when I pressed the button to answer.

"Mrs. Schweitzer?" a female voice inquired.

"Yes," I managed to reply.

"I don't think I have very good news for you."

It's unclear to me if or what I replied.

The voice went on to say, "The test was positive."

It took me a moment to comprehend what I'd heard. Then I screamed and fell to my knees. Didn't the nurse understand the importance of this news? I tried to make her understand this was cause for celebration.

"I thought you had an implant to prevent a pregnancy," she said.

Crying and shaking I thanked her and told her to have Doctor Hovland explain what was going on.

I was still on my knees in the middle of my living room, tears of joy streaming down my face when I hung up the phone. I couldn't believe that Christa's dream was coming true. Marlis, understanding that I wanted privacy to tell Christa, congratulated me and left to share the good news with Mom.

I was so excited I couldn't remember Christa's telephone number even though it was programmed into the phone. I had to look the number up before I could place the call. Christa answered before the first ring finished.

"You're pregnant!" I exclaimed.

"Are you sure? Are you really sure?"

Then we cried and laughed. We were so overcome with emotion that we really didn't say anything significant for several minutes except, "Thank God, thank God. It's a miracle."

When we finally gathered our wits, we talked about how blessed we were.

"Do you suppose you will have morning sickness?" Christa wondered.

I could tell she was concerned about what I would have to endure for her and she felt responsible. I realized that these were the questions I would have been asking her if the roles were reversed. I tried to reassure her that I was and would continue to be fine. I wasn't worried about those small details at all. Finally, we determined who would call whom to share our wondrous news.

Christa wanted to call Curtis and Gina, and also Doctor Phipps and Salina. We divided the rest of the family evenly. Reluctantly, we said goodbye so we could begin making our calls. Brenda started crying, as did several others when I shared our good news.

In the middle of one of the calls it suddenly dawned on me that I needed to get to the pharmacy before they closed to get a progesterone suppository. Doctor Phipps had instructed me that if we got a positive result, I would need to start using these suppositories immediately. They would be used along with other hormone treatments.

I literally ran out of the house and raced to the only pharmacy in town that carried this special suppository. These were not something ordinarily stocked. They had to be handmade by special prescription. I had prearranged for a few to be ready "just in case."

The pharmacist acted entirely too normal and so did an acquaintance I encountered on the way back to my car. I felt like I was a beacon flashing, "A miracle has happened. A miracle has happened." Funny they didn't notice that.

With a humble heart, I went to our church and bowed before the statue of the Virgin Mother. I thanked the Lord and I thanked Mary. The candles I lit were for Curtis, Gina and boys; Christa, Kevin and Justin; Danny and me (for our health), and for the baby.

Arriving back home, I called some of my coworkers who were anxiously awaiting the news. After that, I just leaned back silently thanking God as I shed quiet tears of joy. About an hour later Danny arrived home. When I heard his car I went to the top of the steps.

He took one step in, looked up and said, "Well?"

"Christa is expecting a baby," I answered.

Chapter 19

Are We? Aren't We? And How Many?

Christa shared the news with Kevin via telephone later that night. He had nervously been attending meetings all day. As soon as he was able, he called Christa. When he heard that he was going to be a new daddy, he was ecstatic. He could hardly wait to call his parents, Rosie and Jim Uchytil. But that call had to keep until Kevin arrived home the next night so he and Christa could make the call together.

Curtis and Gina called Danny and me to share in the excitement. They had already talked to Christa twice since the news. Curtis couldn't believe he was actually going to see his mother pregnant again, and Gina exclaimed that she couldn't believe she was going to see her mother-in-law pregnant. We agreed that they should wait to tell the boys after the pregnancy was more advanced.

After a few more calls from siblings, as well as our parents, it was bedtime. I was exhausted but exhilarated. I slept surprisingly well that night, although prayers of thanksgiving floated skyward whenever I stirred.

The next morning my first duty as an expectant grandmother was to buy doughnuts for the teacher's lounge at Simmons Junior High where I worked and for the lounge at Lincoln, my first school where many of my dear friends still worked. I left the doughnuts with a note that read, "There are doughnuts in the lounge for you, from me. Guess who is a Grandma-to-be?"

That day was an exciting one at my school. Friends and coworkers shared in our joy with hugs and congratulations. Everyone was encouraging and supportive. That afternoon I received balloons and warm notes

96

from my close friends at Lincoln School as well as my dear friends at Simmons. The following day I found a jar of home made pickles on my desk. (A few weeks later those pickles came in handy as I sat on my kitchen counter and devoured nearly the entire jar.)

That evening, when Christa and I compared our day, I found that she too had enjoyed a day of warmth and love from friends and work mates. Kevin had sent her flowers and friends had sent her balloons. It was a lovely beginning.

The University of Minnesota needed more than excitement and joy. Doctor Phipps needed actual numbers from my blood test. Salina called wanting to know the exact level of Human Chorionic Gonadotropin (HCG). HCG is secreted by the fertilized embryo and is important in maintaining its viability once it has implanted in the womb. Between the second and third week of gestation HCG levels are usually detectable in a pregnant woman's blood. Throughout the first month of pregnancy the levels rise rapidly.

All I could tell Salina was that the test was positive. This worried me and I felt uneasy. Could this mean a pregnancy hadn't really taken place?

Salina explained that I would need additional blood work. The quantitative HCG number should double with the next test. As Christa and I talked on the phone we were apprehensive and eager for the second blood test which I would have the following day.

Relief changed back into a state of anticipation. On Wednesday, March 7, I was at the hospital bright and early to have my blood drawn before reporting to school. The hospital lab was supposed to call with the results as soon as they were known. While preparing to have this second batch of blood drawn, I inquired about the numbers from the first test. The HCG result was sixty-two. This meant nothing to me, but it gave me a number that I knew needed to double. "Think 124, 124, 124," I repeated to myself. It became my mantra.

I called Salina with that number and she seemed pleased and explained that the first week after conception the range is from five to fifty and this number needs to double within a couple of days. Well, that meant that sixty-two was good.

"Come on 124."

I repeated this in my mind so much it felt like I was at the craps tables, and I've never played.

I stayed at my desk over lunch, and at exactly 12:19 p.m. a technician from the lab called to say my HCG was now at 162.

Eagerly, I called Christa and she called Salina with the terrific news. Later that afternoon, Doctor Phipps called to tell me to begin the folic acid he had prescribed earlier. He was trying to sound so professional but he could not hide the excitement in his voice. It was still early, and as always he didn't want to set us up for heartbreak. The fact is, we had set ourselves up for heartbreak from the moment we entered his office the first time. Each step of progress was another cause for jubilation for us.

During our evening phone report Christa told me, "There's something in Salina's voice that implies there might be more than one baby."

We didn't discuss this other than this brief mention. We were still holding our breaths in hopes that the pregnancy was firmly established. We couldn't think beyond that. Our phone bills really soared as Christa and I talked at least once every day. She needed to keep current on every little detail. Her concern for my health and general well-being was genuine and touching. She felt bad when she learned the patches were irritating. She fretted over the messy suppositories and painful shots. Christa was worried that I would have morning sickness and inquired after my eating habits. Such a mother hen!

I thought everything was going quite well. My work was going great, and since I was drawing plans for new library shelving, I kept myself occupied with that most evenings. Danny and I spent countless hours at the school measuring, planning and designing the shelves to flatter the shape of the library and replace the outdated and unsafe metal shelves. I had free reign of the library design. I wanted to reconfigure it to create a whole new look, and this was right up my alley. I thrive on changing a room, a house or a library!

Just days after learning of the pregnancy I arrived home from work to find a letter from Rosie and Jim Uchytil, Kevin's parents. Eagerly, I opened the envelope and found the most beautiful letter. Tears ran down my cheeks as I read how happy and pleased they both were. Rosie understood our decision perfectly and would have gladly done this herself if she could have.

Rosie and Jim had adopted their own two children so they understood perfectly how the gift of children in a marriage brings joy and fulfillment. She and Jim promised they would pray for my health as well as the health of their unborn grandchild. This letter is something I will treasure forever. Someday it will belong to Chad and Chelsea. They will know that though things were a bit unusual, they were wanted and loved by so many.

Life continued quite normally, except for little things like the lipstick written notes on the bathroom mirrors, reminding me to add or remove the patches on my stomach. After checking my patch charts each night, I wrote the instructions on the bathroom mirror using lipstick or a red marker that washed off. The following morning, after I followed those instructions, I erased them from the mirror. Of course, I still checked and double-checked the charts. This was because I was terrified I'd goof up and ruin everything.

The shots also provided a deviant start to each day. Many times it was just routine. Stick, push plunger, and remove needle. But once in a while there were problems. Like the time Danny wasn't quite awake. After I stuck myself, he pushed on the plunger a moment, then removed the needle. "The oil went in easy today," he said. I looked at the syringe in his hand and was surprised to see most of the oil still in the contraption. He looked at it and said, "Oh, oh. Stick it back in."

Another time, when Danny removed the needle a fine spray of blood misted the dresser and carpeting. He felt terrible but it looked worse then it felt. Then there were the times I'd stick myself and from reflex pull the needle immediately back out without injecting anything in. Danny would always say, "Why did you do that?" To which I had no reply other than, "I don't know. Reflexes?"

Both of my hips were black, blue and sore from the injections, yet I never wished I didn't have to endure them. It was simply part of the procedure and I would have taken them in the bottoms of my feet if that would have made this work. Actually, the patches were more bothersome. My stomach itched and I couldn't find a place without a patch to scratch. The red, sore, sweaty feeling on my tummy was a constant irritation. The patches also kept me panicked that I'd mess up and forget to add or remove the right ones at the right time of day.

The daily injections at seven each morning were over in a minute with nothing more than mild hip discomfort. Occasionally, I would need to enlist the help of one of the teachers or my library assistant with the push of the plunger. Danny was sometimes out of town overnight and try as I might, I could not squeeze that oil through that needle. On those days, I would take my gear and head to school a little early. In the library closet, I'd get my shot for the day. Every few days, Doctor Phipps or Salina would call to see how I was doing.

Doctor Phipps would always say, "Now you should have on patch number 11, 12 and 13."

When I would reply with an affirmative, he'd say, "Good, good. And the shots are going okay?" It was his way of making sure I wasn't forgetting them. It always amazed me that he knew exactly where I was on the charts. Christa and I were always warmed by his calls and genuine concern. We knew he was happy for us and wanted all to go well.

Just twenty-two days after the good news we had a scare. Danny and I were watching the Oscar presentations on television, when I felt a warm gush flow from me. I hurried to the bathroom and stared in horror at blood and tissue pieces in the bathroom stool. In a trance I walked back to my chair.

"I'm afraid I just miscarried the baby," I said.

Danny tried to say comforting words but I was just numb. I did not cry. I just felt hollow. I called Christa and told her I'd had some spotting but I could not tell her how severe it was. If, by some miracle we were still pregnant, I did not want to alarm her unnecessarily.

Early the next morning, I called Doctor Phipps. He instructed me to stay in bed as he tried to be reassuring.

"Sometimes women have some blood loss and still carry a baby to term," he stated. "For your peace of mind though, I think it would be best if you come to see me as soon as possible."

It was just one day before Easter break at school. With very little discussion, we decided we would go to the University the following morning, early. Once more, Christa met us in Brookings so we could travel together the rest of the way. Danny drove and Christa rode up front with him, while I stayed lying down in the back. We chatted mindlessly and I felt that Danny and Christa were oblivious to how worried I actually was.

My thoughts were for Christa and Kevin. My fear was that the letdown would be a tremendous blow, yet I couldn't bring myself to tell her how bad I thought things were. The last hundred miles I intensified my prayers, constantly repeating the *Hail Mary* and *Our Father*, along with the "Please God."

This was by far the longest journey to Minneapolis yet, and when we pulled into the parking garage I was both relieved and terrified. Doctor Phipps saw us immediately after we entered his office, and in a matter of minutes I was lying back prepared for yet another ultrasound. Danny and Christa were with me in the examining room, as the machine and I were readied.

As I was lying there, I made the Sign of the Cross. Then I heard Christa gasp.

"Is that them?" she said.

My eyes flew open, and Christa's gaze locked with mine. I burst into tears. I sobbed so emotionally that Doctor Phipps had to tell me to try to stay still so he could get a clear picture from the ultrasound. My body convulsed with tears of joy and thankfulness.

"How many?" I asked.

"Mom, there are two babies. Look at their hearts beating."

Doctor Phipps turned the monitor so I could see and what an awesome sight it was to see the blink, blink, of those two tiny hearts only days in the womb. Christa was so excited, Danny was happy, and I was relieved. Doctor Phipps was all business as usual. He fiddled with the monitor, measuring gestational sacs and explaining what he thought had occurred.

A third cystic structure was present and Dr. Phipps explained that this may have been a third embryo that did not stay attached to the uterine wall. At the time we were so thrilled to still be pregnant and to find out there were two, that we did not mourn the loss of the third. We remembered that Doctor Phipps had explained that fertilized eggs do not always result in pregnancies. Some attach to the uterine wall and continue to develop. Others do not. This was normal.

After I was dressed, we all visited about our hasty and anxiety-filled trip. Doctor Phipps relaxed a bit and smiled at our happiness. He explained that Salina was out of town. She would be disappointed that she had missed us and wasn't present to share our fantastic news. We knew she would be just as happy for us as members of our own family.

Christa, always concerned about what she was putting her parents through, inquired about our sex life! She openly asked Doctor if we could now safely resume relations. Doctor thought not. After this scare it was best to refrain and give these babies every chance possible. This was only moderately embarrassing. After all we'd been through together, it seemed natural to face the fact that married couples do have sex, including one's parents – and for that matter, one's children. Privately, I was concerned about this twist. Yet I knew Danny, like me, would do anything for his grandchildren, born or unborn.

After a few more instructions and a warm goodbye, we left the clinic. It was nearly three in the afternoon, just enough time to call my school and tell the secretary and Pam the wonderful news. I wanted them to be able to spread the word before the Easter break because so many people on the staff were concerned about this complication. I made the call from a pay phone right outside the clinic doors. Christa did not call Kevin, she wanted to tell him in person. Relief and happiness was the response from the school. Now it was time to start for home. We had a long trip ahead of us and the following day would be another extremely long trip for Christa and Kevin.

It was a family tradition to go to Danny's parents' house for Easter. The trip from Sioux City to Lemmon is four hundred and seventy-miles, and that meant that Christa would be in a vehicle for nearly thirteen hundred miles in two days. Yet, she would have lots of festive news to share with the relatives in Lemmon. It would be fun!

The trip back to Brookings was a happy time of speculation. Would there be two boys, two girls, or one of each. Christa did not care about their sex, just so they were healthy. We were nearly dizzy with the news.

We left Christa off at her car. After refueling both vehicles, we said our goodbyes and drove off in separate directions. I watched Christa's car for as long as I could. It was always hard for me to see her travel by herself, and it would be dark before she arrived home. I would be glad to hear she was home safe and sound. When we arrived back in Aberdeen, our odometer told us we had driven seven hundred and eighty miles that day. It had been worth it, and had been an immense relief. There were two babies and we were doubly blessed!

Christa had fun telling Kevin about their new condition. Kevin greeted her with a "What's happening?"

Christa deliberately replied, "They're fine."

Thinking he was about to become a father of four little babies at once Kevin, could hardly spit out, "How many?"

Christa and Kevin celebrated the good news with a warm toast to their babies' future as they looked over the ultrasound pictures Doctor Phipps had sent with Christa. Easter was especially wonderful. Christa was proudly showing all the relatives her babies' pictures. Everyone was delighted that there were two.

Lucas, Clay and Cole would touch my tummy and try to "feel Christa's babies." The boys were not the least bit puzzled by what was happening. They understood perfectly that Christa did not have that special place where the baby eggs grow. They knew Gramma was going to keep Christa and Kevin's babies warm and safe until they were ready to be born. It was as simple as that. Now instead of the birds and the bees, there were the birds, bees and the butterflies in action.

Back at school, I was also showing off pictures of my newest grandchildren. Two! I couldn't get over the wonder of this. The dream just kept getting better!

I doubled my efforts to eat right and drink twice as much milk and water. I read everything I could on prenatal care and did my best to do everything right for these babies. I felt so responsible and worried over every little discomfort. It was really difficult to believe that there actually were babies in there. It just didn't seem real. I wanted a sign that they were all right. I continued to pray for their well being, lighting two candles now instead of the one for baby. I also did crazy little things, like always taking an even number of swallows of water and bites of food. This was a childish gesture, like not stepping on a sidewalk crack. But with two babies, taking five sips of water seemed to be cheating. It was really just a game I played for myself, but it kept me aware of the need to drink a lot of water for two.

In April, we had our final appointment with Doctor Phipps. We scheduled it over spring break on the 19th. It was amazing how our appointments continued to coincide with breaks at school. This helped to save my sick days for the birth of the babies. Danny and I would meet Christa

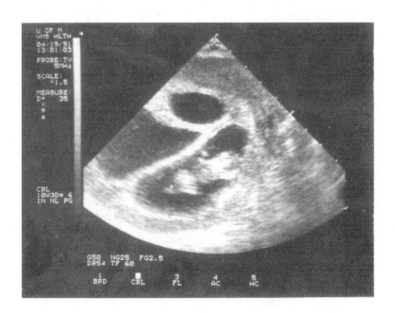

Chelsea and Chad's baby picture taken on April 19, 1991.

and Kevin at the University, then go to Sioux City for the weekend. We were excited for this checkup. I needed confirmation because I was still suffering from "it can't be real" anxiety.

Kevin was excited about his chance to see the babies for the first time and Christa was just bursting with happiness. Salina was waiting for us with hugs and congratulations.

It was pure joy to see the two babies on the screen that day. They were much bigger and quite active. Again the blinkity-blink of their tiny hearts brought tears to our eyes. It was a profound moment for us. This time our goodbyes were a little sad. The subsequent checkups were going to be done in Aberdeen with an obstetrician there.

We hugged Salina and Doctor Phipps and tried to convey how we felt about them and all they had done for us. It was not easy. How do you thank someone for helping your daughter become a mother? Their efforts were allowing Christa and Kevin to be parents together. None of us thought of this as making medical history. We were just grateful for their role in giving us new little lives to love and nurture.

Chapter 19

Word of Our Miracle Spreads

May Day 1991 started off beautifully. In the morning I received a May basket from Bryan Delzer. No, this wasn't a secret love. Bryan is a young man who was a classmate of Christa's in grade school. He is also a former neighbor boy.

In 1972, when Bryan was about four years old, he brought a May basket to our door. Christa was too shy to chase him at that age, so I did. In keeping with the May Day tradition I gave him a big kiss on the cheek. Every May Day since that one in 1972, Bryan has brought a May basket to our home. Attending college out of the state and even marriage has not stopped the baskets. It is a delightful way to celebrate the beginning of Spring from a delightful young man.

It was a gorgeous spring day and I felt vibrant with life as I entered the clinic. It was my first appointment with a local obstetrician and I had never met him before. Doctor Hovland had been my gynecologist for 23 years. He had delivered Christa and Chad plus two of Curtis' boys. Although he was still in practice, he had stopped delivering babies just the previous year. This was a baleful disappointment for me. To change doctors after all these years was not going to be easy.

Doctor Carlson and Doctor Berry practiced together and Doctor Hovland's advice was to choose either. "They are both good," he said. I had never even laid eyes on either so I chose by the scientific method of "eeny, meeny." Doctor Carlson's nurse, Angie, came into the examining room with her clipboard and started asking me questions. "What was the date of my last period?" was her first. Immediately, I was faced with the task of explaining this unusual pregnancy.

I began by saying, "This is going to sound strange, but that question really isn't relevant. You see, I am pregnant but these are my daughter's babies."

Angie's face turned red but she beamed with understanding. "This is wonderful!" she exclaimed.

I continued to explain all that had happened and where we were in the pregnancy. She took notes for a few moments then left to get Doctor Carlson. Doctor Carlson is a terrific looking man but I honestly didn't notice that first. He was just very nice and that's what I noticed. We visited about the pregnancy and about Christa and Kevin before he examined me. I explained that often the parents will come with me for these checkups. We also talked about the risks and possible problems that could occur.

Dr. Carlson understood perfectly when I told him we wanted Christa's and Kevin's names on the birth certificates. He nodded as I explained that I was merely incubating these babies and the moment they were born they would be Uchytils. I wanted Christa to wear the wrist bracelet matching the babies. I also wanted her to share the hospital room with me (if the hospital agreed), and for her to have all the new mom privileges. The doctor and I were in perfect agreement in all areas. I was going to like this man.

During the physical exam, Doctor Carlson told me I wasn't his oldest patient, but that I was his most unique one. He thought I was in fine health and everything looked perfectly normal. When I delivered my own children, my labor had been relatively short. A natural delivery would be the goal once more. The examination included a Doppler to hear the babies' heartbeats. This was a wonderful sound and another assurance that the babies were alive and well. Doctor Carlson thought it best if he saw me every two weeks. At the next visit he planned to do an ultrasound. I explained that there would be quite a crowd for this event.

Our due date was November 15, just seven days after my forty-third birthday. Actually I always thought of this as Christa's due date. I never said, "I'm due on November 15." Even now, I talk about when Christa was expecting the twins. I might say "when I was carrying the twins" if the conversation is directly related to that time.

Doctor Carlson went on to explain that the babies needed to stay in the womb for at least thirty-four weeks in order to have the best chance of survival. Christa and Kevin planned to come to Aberdeen for as many appointments as possible, and of course Danny would be there also. Doctor Carlson was very receptive to these unorthodox arrangements. His understanding was a relief and a comfort to us. Another hurdle had been jumped.

After leaving the doctor's office, I went directly to the church as always. My thanks that day included a special thank-you for finding Dr. Carlson. I knew he would help us make this time as special for Christa and Kevin as it should be. Next I went home and immediately marked October 4 on the calendar. That would be the thirty-four-week mark. The date was like a milestone to be reached. "Please let these babies stay inside me for at least that many weeks," I prayed.

I then circled every Friday on the calendar and wrote the week – week four, week five, and so on. Each Friday was a mini-goal to reach. One more week of growth, one more week closer to being viable outside the womb. Our call to Christa that night was full of news about Doctor Carlson and Angie. Christa was eager to meet "our new doctor," especially after I teased Danny by telling Christa that labor would be a snap because, "boy do I have a focal point – Doctor Carlson!"

The first week in May we started getting calls from the media. The local newspapers and television stations wanted interviews about the pregnancy. It wasn't easy to keep saying "no." These were local people in our community and we hated to disappoint them. Yet, we had no intention of making this a public affair. Life continued very normally most of the time. We still had to work and do household chores. We also spent time talking to our grandsons.

Danny was scheduled for a recheck of his colon on Friday, May 3. An outpatient colonoscopy procedure was scheduled with our family doctor. Doctor Janusz thought Danny's colon looked better than the last checkup. Danny felt that our good news had actually helped him improve. This was especially good news for me, as I worried that the added stress and worry about me would actually aggravate his ulcerative colitis.

After Danny's appointment and after the school day ended, we left for Rapid City to visit Curtis, Gina and our three Grandsons. We had a wonderful time. The weather was gorgeous and the Black Hills seemed especially beautiful. We always crammed so much into those weekends with Lucas' soccer games, church, scenic drives and visiting. My brother, Cliff, and his wife also live in Rapid City, and many times they would join us. We are an extremely close family, and Cliff and Zada are an important part of that extended family.

That weekend, as we watched the boys cavort, we enjoyed speculating on Christa and Kevin's babies. We agreed that health was of primary importance, but it was fun to guess about what gender each baby would be. As the conversation seemed to revolve around me, I realized how unreal it all seemed. Christa was going to be a mother. Our rocket was on the way to the moon!

The second week in May, Salina called from the University and asked us if we would do a segment for a Minneapolis television station. The station was doing a three-part program on infertility featuring Doctor Phipps and the clinic. We agreed, mostly because we wanted to do something to repay Doctor Phipps and the University for our miracle. Christa and I went shopping the night before the taping. I was beginning to outgrow my blouses and I wanted something that would cover my tummy but not look like a maternity top. This unusual situation proved to be a unique mother/daughter shopping trip.

The team of three reporters and camera people flew into Sioux City and spent most of the day with us. It was a very cold and windy Saturday. The actual interview took several hours. They asked some probing questions of all of us. This was our first taste of working with broadcast media, and we didn't realize how many hours of taping were required to produce a few minutes of television programming. The station sent us a copy of the mini-series and it was wonderful. It was a tastefully done segment and we were proud of the finished product.

At home in Aberdeen, the media calls started coming more often. Time after time I turned reporters down. Still, the circle widened. Calls started coming from farther and farther away. One reporter in North Dakota got really angry with me.

"You're denying people in your own backyard access to information that people as far away as South America have," he told me.

What? This was news to me. He needed to explain himself. The reporter went on to tell me that a journalism student from South America had been at the University of Minnesota and saw the special on infertility. She planned to write an article about our situation as soon as she got back to South America. This North Dakota reporter overheard the student telling someone at some convention, or in a cab or somewhere. I was too shocked to catch all of what he was saying.

In the beginning it had not occurred to us that there would be public or media interest in our story. We could understand interest on the part of families with infertility problems like Christa's wanting to learn more about us – but South America? Needless to say, the reporter's tenor did little to persuade me. It just made me determined not to talk to him.

Danny and I discussed this new twist that evening. We also called Christa and Kevin to fill them in. Everyone agreed that we would continue to keep this a family affair. And for the next two months we did just that. Christa and Kevin were coming regularly to our Doctor appointments, especially if an ultrasound was planned. It was so fun to watch those two squeal and hug each other with delight as the babies moved. Danny and I were in awe of this ability to view unborn babies too. What a joy it was to watch your grandchildren develop from that blinking heart beat on the monitor into discernible human forms measuring two, four and then six inches long. At just two inches they already looked like miniature newborns. What an experience it was to observe their development! Danny and I would grow misty-eyed watching Christa. She fairly danced with excitement as she viewed her babies.

At one of these appointments in June, Christa called out, "I see a penis."

Kevin, Dan and I were incredulous, but Doctor Carlson agreed. One baby was definitely a boy. The other baby was being very discreet and did not offer us a view that helped discern gender. Christa and Kevin were delighted, they hugged and clapped. Danny and I were thrilled too. We love our grandsons very much. Another was more than fine with us. Simply because we had no granddaughters, we thought it would be nice if the other baby was a girl.

These checkups were a needed mental support to me. When Doctor Carlson pointed out anatomical features like their little spines, kidneys, the four chambers of their hearts and other vital organs, I just sighed with relief. I would have gone in everyday just to hear him say, "Everything is fine, both babies are still gaining weight and growing."

Each time I felt an unusual twinge or ache, I went on high alert. I longed for the babies to start moving enough that I could feel it and know they were okay. Yet I worried that Christa would be saddened because she couldn't experience this milestone. Even though she had assured me that she felt only joy, I was concerned her heart might ache for what she was missing. God took care of this, too. One afternoon as Christa, Danny and I were talking on the phone, I felt the first stir of the babies. "Christa" I whispered, "your babies just moved."

It was a wonderful moment, as shared as it could be. When the three of us talked on the phone, I often held my receiver on my tummy so the twins could hear Christa's voice. Christa and I had both read about potential bonding with the voice before birth. Neither of us were really worried about the babies' bond with Christa. For one thing, our voices are very alike. But this was just one more way we could facilitate that bond.

In June, Danny and I spent some time in Rapid City. Danny was helping Curtis take a wall out to enlarge their living room. Normally I would have been right in the midst of this with a hammer. Now I sat and watched the activity from a safe distance. Curtis, Gina and the boys were surprised at how the babies were growing. My tummy now stuck out and it was obvious that I was pregnant. The boys kept trying to feel the babies and would put their heads to my tummy trying to hear them. They were a delight.

When quizzed about who was going to have a baby, they always answered, "Christa and Kevin." Never once did they say "Gramma." To them, this was as natural as any pregnancy. It wasn't that easy for others or on occasion, me. Carrying babies, but not expecting them, can create strange situations. Once while I was shopping for maternity clothes a young women was looking at the same rack as I. We exchanged glances, then timid greetings as strangers often do . After a while she asked me how far along I was. She was the same. Then she inquired about who the doctor was that I was seeing, and I asked her about her general wellbeing.

After a few more polite exchanges, she asked, "Is this your first child?"

I hedged. Should I fudge and make this painless, or tell the truth and not be able to fully explain? I opted for the truth.

"I have two children," I answered.

"How old are they?" the young mother-to-be inquired.

"Twenty-two and twenty-six," I replied. "These babies are my daughter's children. She can't carry them so I am doing it for her."

The young woman looked at me, eyes filled with astonishment. Then she nodded and hugged me. "That is so awesome," she exclaimed. "I think you're wonderful."

She wished me luck, then hurried away without buying anything. I smiled and glowed a bit, too. That wasn't so hard and she understood without much of an explanation. Good!

The time was fast approaching when Danny and I would need to start sharing this venture. Our friends and family knew. Our colleagues knew. But what about the people in our community we knew in a less familiar context? There were the folks we saw every week in church, but only recognized them by sight and did not know by name. There were people we greeted at the post office, the grocery store, the gas station. I was starting to get looks. Those sidelong looks that said, "Um... she looks pregnant. Aren't their children married and gone? Are those two starting a second family?"

Danny and I had discussed this. How do you tell the people you don't really know well? We didn't want people thinking we had a baby, and then gave it away. We had a dilemma.

Danny started to consider the idea of talking to our local paper and thought that letting them do an interview would answer a lot of questions in one shot. I tended to agree. Kevin was the most reluctant to have any publicity at all. He is a very private person and opening up to strangers was not something he felt comfortable doing, but he understood our dilemma and agreed that a local interview might be necessary.

Christa and Kevin were telling their friends about the pregnancy. To help her inform acquaintances, I bought her a tee-shirt and had two babies put on it with the words "Mother to Be." She loved it.

When I told my sister, Darlene, about the calls from the media, she felt we should give our story to at least one prestigious magazine. She had remarried and with husband, Ron, she wrote a letter to the editor of *Life Magazine*. Within days, the magazine contacted her and wanted to talk with us. A nice gentleman who identified himself as an editor explained that the magazine would like to send a photographer out and would do an exclusive photo session for the magazine. He went on to explain that this would be strictly a photo session for news purposes. *Life Magazine*, like most legitimate periodicals, does not pay any money for feature stories.

After much discussion and uncertainty, we agreed to meet the photographer. Tom flew to Aberdeen to spend several days with us. He went with us to the doctor and saw an ultrasound for the first time. He asked the doctor about natural birth versus birth with the administration of medications. Before Doctor Carlson could answer, Danny piped up with, "You're in South Dakota, Tom. We'll just give Arlette a bullet to bite on."

Doctor Carlson spun around on his chair saying, "No! No! We have all the modern equipment and medicines." You could tell just what he was thinking – *Life Magazine* writing about South Dakotans giving birth in a covered wagon or some other primitive scenario.

Tom was very amiable, so it was natural to have him join us for a barbecue on our patio. It was splendid hearing about his trips and the people he had photographed. Just before coming to photograph us he had been on assignment to Medjugorje, the holy site in the former Yugoslavia. Many people had made pilgrimages based on reports of visions of the Blessed Mother and miraculous cures. That was of particular interest to me. Tom's retelling of his experience there was so detailed we felt he had transported us to the very site.

Tom had also photographed many famous people and we were impressed and somewhat flattered that he had been selected to photograph us. The day he left Aberdeen, the two of us had lunch at a local restaurant. Our waitress knew me slightly and inquired, "What's new, Arlette?"

"Not much," I replied, "but I'm enjoying my summer."

When she walked away Tom said, "Not much? Here you are, having lunch with a photographer from *Life Magazine*, you're carrying your daughter's children, about to make medical history in the United States – and you say not much?"

We shared a good laugh over that. I hadn't given it a thought. When Tom left later that day, I drove him to the airport. I told him we were undecided about doing an exclusive interview. Our family had several conversations about going public and we were still hesitant to do so. We agreed that *Life* was a reputable, respected magazine. Yet, if we did agree to have them write about our experience they would not want even our local paper to get the story. I could not promise anything. If we went public, we felt an obligation to our town's paper. This was all so new to us. We wanted to do the right thing.

In July, Lucas, Clay and Cole came for their summer visit. We had ten days of fun. We went to the parks, played games, and went swimming at the municipal pool. The children's pool was crowded with young mothers and one pregnant grandma. I got quite a few sidelong looks as I waded with Cole and Clay. Danny and I also took the two younger boys in the big pool along with Lucas to enjoy the deeper water. It was easy and comforting to carry the boys in the water and this was nice because I didn't dare try to carry them otherwise. We made a mini vacation out of the trip back to Rapid City to return the boys to Curtis and Gina. We took in the sightseeing spots, the Badlands east of Rapid City at Wall, and stayed in a hotel.

The hotel had a lovely outdoor pool so we spent a couple days letting the boys enjoy the water. One evening after a swim I was letting the three little guys get a soda out of a machine. A lady came by, ruffled

Cole's head and said to me, "I bet you're hoping this one's a girl honey." I couldn't wait to tell Danny that. Unknowingly that lady she had given me a beautiful compliment.

For our actual vacation that summer we reserved a large cabin in the Black Hills. Curtis, Gina and the boys as well as Christa, Kevin and Justin were joining us for a few days of fun and relaxation. The year before, all ten of us had taken Curtis' van to Seattle for a family wedding. After the wedding festivities we rented a house on the ocean where we had a marvelous time.

The house we rented had four bedrooms and came complete with a hot tub on the deck. The forest surrounded the cabin and it was magnificent. The four boys played endlessly and we all hiked a bit, (I tired easily). Christa was interested in the pregnancy. She looked at my swelling belly and examined the line that develops during pregnancy. She was happy yet somewhat wistful. I wished it were her. When I told her that she exclaimed, "Mom, I'm not one bit jealous! I'm just so happy, so it really is fine with me. We are so very grateful that the Lord has blessed us so."

This conversation made me feel much better. After that wonderful weekend ended we followed Christa and Kevin back to their home in Sioux City, Iowa. Christa wanted Danny and I to meet the people she worked with. Danny still had vacation days so off we went. Christa's coworkers all thought what we were doing was wonderful.

While we were in Sioux City, we were contacted by staff of the NBC Nightly News with Tom Brokaw. This was big. Tom Brokaw is a South Dakota boy and because of that connection it was tempting to do a segment for his program. We discussed and relized we were not going to keep the story quiet forever. Besides we all liked Tom Brokaw, so we ultimately decided we would do a story with him. The producer agreed not to break the story before we had a chance to talk to our local papers. Christa and Kevin were coming to Aberdeen the second week in August for another checkup. We would talk to our local paper then.

The last week in July, I had a bit of a jolt. After meeting some of my school friends for lunch I went to my scheduled doctor's appointment. My plan was to take my mother grocery shopping afterward. After Doctor Carlson examined me he sat back with a little sigh.

"I think the time has come for you to be on bed rest," he said.

I gasped and covered my face with my hands. "Is something wrong with the babies?" I asked.

"The babies look fine," he assured me. "But your cervix seems to be

113

thinning a bit. I don't want to take any chances with these premium babies."

"I agree," I said. "But do you mean total bed rest? What about my job?" I was due back at work in about three weeks.

Doctor Carlson said, "Let's take one step at a time. For now, I want you on modified bed rest. You can move from the couch to the recliner to the bed. As long as things go okay you can eat meals at the table and occasionally go out for a quick lunch or a movie.

"However, the goal is to make sure there is good blood exchange with the placenta. So I want you to spend most of your time lying down, preferably on your right side."

At this point I had weekly appointments, so he encouraged me by saying, "If nothing changes over the next couple of weeks, I might give you permission to go back to work."

I hadn't bargained on bed rest, but I knew I would be good at it! I love to read, work crosswords and jigsaw puzzles. I would keep myself entertained. My sister, Darlene, was coming for a visit and that would also help. We would laugh our way though the first week, plus I would enjoy her cooking. But I was concerned about my job. Starting a new school year was not something a substitute could easily do. All the new materials that have been ordered need to be processed and put on the shelves. Just readying the library for the students was a monumental task. Poor Pam, my assistant. We depended on each other to accomplish the myriad tasks that needed to be completed before the students returned.

When I left Doctor Carlson's office, I didn't go straight home as he had directed. I made my usual stop at the church. This was much more than a ritual. It gave me strength and hope. My prayers were for the health of the two precious lives that I had the privilege of carrying. Realizing for the first time that premature labor was a real possibility, I fervently prayed they would stay put until they were ready to be born.

What if I moved too much, or walked too far or sat too long? If I went into labor I would feel so guilty. I had taken my own pregnancies for granted. All of our children were practically ten-month babies. My activities were never restricted. In fact, with my other pregnancies I had shoveled snow and had snow ball fights in my ninth month. After my visit to the Church, I went directly home, I did not pass go, I did not collect any money. I also did not take my mother shopping.

Chapter 21

Media, Media and More Media

Thursday morning, August 1, I was awakened by the telephone ringing. It was a woman who identified herself as a reporter with the *New York Times*. She had heard of our story and the *Times* planned to publish a story in their Sunday or Monday issue. The reporter hoped Christa and I would give her an interview, but regardless they were going ahead with the story.

I told the woman I would call her back because I wanted to talk with Danny and Christa before I committed to anything. Danny wasn't disturbed by this turn of events. He felt that if the *New York Times* already had the story, we should do an interview to ensure they had our side of it. After calling Christa it was decided. Christa agreed that if the story was going to be printed, it should be as factual as possible. We also decided to call our local newspaper, the *Aberdeen American News*, and give them the opportunity to scoop the *Times*.

Within hours a photographer was at our house and a reporter was on the way to Christa's home. A reporter from the *American News* called me and we completed an interview over the phone on Friday. The *News* would publish the story in their Sunday edition. This over, we all thought the media attention would subside once the stories were published. We hadn't forgotten our conversation with the people from *NBC Nightly News with Tom Brokaw*. We still planned to go ahead with an interview with him, but thought that would be the extent of our celebrity.

All summer my sister, Darlene, and I had been contriving to have a week together for some fun and laughs. We settled on the first week in

August. Darlene is a comfortable third wheel at our house. Danny, Darlene and I enjoy each other's company immensely. While Danny is at work the two of us gossip and giggle the day away. The Grandchildren's visits were over for the summer and no other company was expected. Darlene and I had planned and plotted to spend time together without interruptions. Were we in for a surprise.

Darlene arrived the same day as the call from the *New York Times*. It was the day our lives took a fork in the road. We had no concept of how different life would be from that day forward. Darlene, Mom, Marlis and Jack (my brother from Lemmon) along with Danny and I, spent the first weekend in August enjoying family time together. I spent most of time lying on the couch. Sunday night, we all went to the movie. Doctor Carlson said that I could take in an occasional movie and this was my first outing since bed rest was ordered.

We were still talking about the movie as we walked into the house about 11:30 pm. I settled into my customary position on the sofa when the phone began ringing. As Danny handed me the phone he mouthed, "It's *Good Morning America*."

The caller was Lori Beecher, one of the producers for the *Good Morning America* show. She had read our story in the early edition of the *New York Times* and wanted us to fly to New York as soon as possible to do the show. When I declined she said she would call back the next day. After hanging up Danny said, "I am so excited I don't think I'll sleep."

Darlene and I chided him about just liking Joan Lundon. The next morning, the phone woke us at about five. I picked up the receiver and the caller said, "This is W_ _ _ radio and we want you to do an on-air interview with us."

I replied, What I want is to go back to sleep. Please call later."

Just as I hung up, the phone rang again. It was a newspaper somewhere in British Columbia. Again I hung up, and again it rang. Danny decided to take the garage phone off the hook so we could sleep.

That morning Danny left for work around eight and Darlene and I got up a short while later. As soon as I put the phone back on the hook it rang in my hand and from that moment on it never stopped for weeks. Darlene started taking the calls as I reclined like a queen on the couch. It was fun to listen to her talk to all these people. She was a natural press agent, taking all the information then reporting to me. The two of us could only visit when the phone was off the hook. Calls were coming from all over the world. Newspapers, radio stations, television shows, magazines and movie producers – it was surreal!

About 11:30 that morning Danny came rushing home to tell me I had forgotten to put the phone back on the hook. Christa had been trying to call me all morning and could only get a busy signal. She had been contacted by media before she left for work and she wanted to discuss those calls with me. Also, she told her dad that Doctor Phipps wanted to talk with me and he could not get through either.

Danny told Christa about our early morning media barrage. He told her he would come home and replace the forgotten receiver. Little did he know that the receiver had been replaced, several times. Incredibly, the

My t-shirt read "Star In The Making." Little did we know that a media barrage awaited us.

calls were continuous. As soon as the receiver was placed back in the cradle, the telephone would ring. Danny was amazed when he saw and heard what was happening. There simply was not enough time between calls for us to even dial out. Could this be happening?

Big names were trying to reach us. *Nightline* with Barbara Walters hosting, Dan Rather, Maury Povich, *Larry King Live*, *Oprah*, *Geraldo*, *The Donahue Show*, Sally Jesse Raphael, *People* and *Time* magazine, and the list went on. Radio stations from across the nation wanted interviews as did newspapers and magazines from around the world.

I talked to no one. I was on bed rest and I just enjoyed the circus from the sidelines. Darlene was wonderful. She could talk to the media and handle the calls like a professional screener. Later that day, Jack, Marlis and Mom stopped over. The atmosphere was electric and they, too, were caught up in the excitement. We pored over the ever-growing list of callers with wonder.

That evening we took the receiver off the hook once again, so we could make some decisions without interruptions. First, we needed to talk to Christa and Kevin because we always collaborated on all decisions. After several tries we finally got through to them late that evening. By this time, their telephone was nearly as busy as ours. We compared lists then decided we would interview with the reporters from *Time* and *People* magazines and do interviews with our local television news shows. I would do some radio interviews because they did not involve any effort. I could lie on the sofa in my robe, and talk away.

There was no denying it – the dike had broken. We could no longer hold back the flood of news that was going to be published and broadcast. We could only try to control the flow by disclosing the facts. Darlene made the arrangements with *Time* and *People* magazines. The reporters would arrive already the next day. I slept soundly until interrupted around two in the morning. Calls started coming from countries in completely different time zones. I would just say, "It is two or three or whatever time it was and hang up." I needed my sleep. Once again we had to resort to the phone off the hook ruse. We did not like to do this in case of an emergency but we had no choice.

Tuesday, Danny left early for work. Darlene and I stayed in bed until around eight. We sauntered into the living room in our nightgowns. The sight in the yard was a jolt. There were vans and cables and trucks and reporters. We both dropped to the floor and looked at each other and started laughing.

"What do we do now?" I shouted, as the doorbell began to ring and the dog started to bark. We just lay there and giggled and giggled. Finally we crawled off to the bathrooms and showered. We just let the doorbell ring.

It was nearly a hour later when Darlene finally answered the bell. Opening the door that day was akin to opening Pandora's box. We were inundated with reporters from around the world. It seemed as though everyone was interested in this story. A grandmother giving birth to her own grandchildren? How is this possible? Why are they doing it? What are people thinking about it? Is this ethical?

What we did not realize was that the front page of the *New York*

Times is what drives other media into action. I cannot describe how weird it is to turn on the television and hear your name and circumstances described on CNN. News stories about a South Dakota grandmother giving birth to her own grandchildren were being broadcast around the globe. It seemed that representatives from every medium, and from every state and country, wanted the "real story."

I would be lying if I said this was not exciting. It was. Yet, we did not want this story sullied. We felt it was a beautiful story of love, faith family and parenthood – not a theatrical act. We did not want our story or our lives sensationalized. First and foremost concern was the well-being of the babies. Second came getting the truthful story out to the public. Third in importance was interviewing with reputable news people and still trying to be fair to those that wanted the story.

Time magazine's reporter was J. Madeline Nash. I liked her immediately. I surprised myself by being completely relaxed throughout the interview. It was easy to just answer every question as honestly as possible. We chatted like two women friends over coffee (water for me.) It was during this interview that I coined the phase "Now we have the birds and the bees and the butterflies too." When I see this on yard signs now, I have to smile because I really believe it had not been used before it extemporaneously came out of my mouth on that day in August 1991.

The reporter for *People* magazine came from Minneapolis, Minnesota. We were immediately at ease with Margaret. The complete interview was done while I remained on my left side, in my robe, on the living room couch. Unfortunately, we were continually interrupted by the doorbell.

It was during the *People* interview that a persistent tabloid writer was videotaped by Darlene. Darlene told this reporter repeatedly that we were not interviewing with any tabloid papers. Undeterred, he parked himself on our front doorstep. Danny arrived home and drove into our garage. Just as he walked into the house, the doorbell began to ring once again.

"This guy won't take 'no' for an answer," Darlene exclaimed.

Dan said, "I'll handle him."

I could hear, but could not see the exchange as Danny explained we were not interested in an interview. With the video camera on, Darlene was able to record audio of the man offering Dan $5,000 on the spot if we would talk to him. When Dan turned him down he increased his offer in increments until he was at $25,000. As Danny was saying "no thanks"

119

Darlene panned the camera on me saying, "Twenty-five thousand dollars!!"

Dan was a cookie salesman and I was a school librarian. This would have been a serious windfall. Later, when this and other tabloids printed stories about us I called this reporter and asked for the money. He said that I hadn't given them an interview so "tough luck." My advice: if money is offered take it. The story will be written regardless.

The media frenzy continued from early August until the end of September. It tapered off until the birth of the twins when it erupted once again. We found most of the media representatives were ethical and honest. But a few were disingenuous. There was one major news program that was particularly disappointing. A crew from the CBS/Dan Rather news team came to Aberdeen. We explained that we had made a verbal promise with the Tom Brokaw/NBC producers that they would have first crack if we decided to a television interview. Because the CBS team had all their equipment and people in town already, they implored us to tape the interview with the condition that they would hold it until after the Tom Brokaw interview aired. We stupidly thought everyone meant what they said. What a shock it was when our piece aired that night.

Another time, a newspaper reporter from South Dakota sold my picture and story to *Playboy* magazine. I was terribly upset when I heard about this. I am conservative by nature and do not approve of the exploitation of women in "girlie" magazines. We contacted our dear friend and attorney, Rory King about this and sued the newspaper reporter. Shortly after, we learned that photographs of me were being sold by many photographers. It didn't bother me when a decent magazine ran a picture and a story. I could even tell from the picture which photographer had sold it. This happened with *Newsweek*, *Women's World* and many foreign magazines as well. Though most magazines do not pay for a story, many will pay a professional photographer for a picture. So if someone made a little money we did not mind.

One British paper offered us a payment for pictures taken after the twins were born and we agreed. By this time we had learned that we had become something of a cottage industry and many were making money on our story. Later, Christa and I both wrote about our experience with a writer for *Ladies' Home Journal* and we were both paid for that story. I'm pleased to say we were thrilled with the article and pictures.

Many people thought we were getting rich as a result of all this media attention. Nothing could have been further from the truth. Newspapers and broadcast media do not pay for news. As I said before, the news magazines do not pay. Most of the other magazines composed their articles from the newspaper reports supplementing them with pictures purchased from photographers. None of the television talk shows pay a nickel. They will pay for your travel expenses and accommodations while you are away from home but there are no honoraria. The money from the British paper and *Ladies' Home Journal* didn't come close to covering the expense of the *in vitro*, let alone make us wealthy!

During all this craziness we also had movie producers courting us. Many flew to South Dakota to talk to us in person. One Hollywood producer used the stereotypical line "My people will talk with your people."

I had to laugh as I replied, "We're it! You're talking to our people."

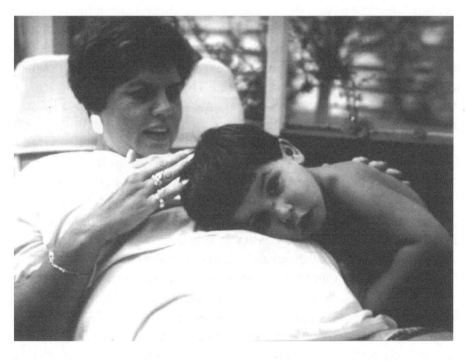

Cole listens for his cousins. Our grandchildren took everything in stride and looked forward to the birth of the twins.

Chap 21

Bedrest Until Birth

As the pregnancy progressed, we knew one of the babies was smaller than the other. Doctor Carlson was closely monitoring the situation, but we didn't realize how serious that can be. I knew he took meticulous and frequent measurements, but we felt he just wanted to see how much the babies were growing. His major concern was that one baby was taking needed nourishment from the other. When he confided that information to us we started to become concerned. Now we not only worried about carrying these babies to the 34-week mark, we worried about them both getting the nourishment they needed to survive and be healthy.

There was nothing I could do but continue to eat right, drink the right fluids, and follow doctor's orders. Other than my appointments with the doctor I rarely left the house until the approach of school. In mid-August, school personnel started to meet and plan for the upcoming year. Doctor Carlson thought it would be safe for me to go back to school as long I sat at my desk and took a break every two hours to lie down.

With the consent of my principal, Danny put a cot in my storage closet for my breaks. This was unconventional to say the least. But it was concluded that it was better to have an encumbered librarian than a substitute who could not dictate what needed to be done. I held up rather well for the first few weeks taking my allotted breaks in the closet. It did get increasingly difficult to roll off the cot once I was down. My swollen belly hindered my movements more each day. It was obvious the babies were growing rapidly now. I just hoped they were both getting the nourishment they needed.

I found myself tiring more quickly and I remember looking at the floor at one staff meeting, and longing to lie down right then and there. My school day ended as soon as the kids left the building. At home I went straight to bed and rested until the next morning. Things seemed to be going fine until a fateful day in mid-September when I nearly shattered our delicate dream.

I had decided to attend an important early-afternoon meeting with my library colleagues and the superintendent of schools to go over budgets and policies. At the conclusion of the meeting, I started down the long hall to go to my car when I felt a painful tug in my crotch. My head swiveled each way as I tried to locate the closest chair or place to rest. I could only go forward and get to my car as quickly as my painful and slow steps would allow.

My mind was reeling and I kept chiding myself, "How could I have been so foolish? No meeting, no job could be so important that it was worth risking the babies' lives."

I was so afraid and miserable, and not a soul was in sight. I realized that I had gotten myself into this situation and that I would have to muster the tenacity and focus to get out of it. My swollen belly coupled with the pressure exerted by gravity made me feel like my bottom was falling out. Moving with weighted feet through air that seemed to have a resistance of its own I realized I'd forgotten to put the eggs ahead of the jelly beans. I hoped God would give me a second chance for the babies' sake.

What seemed like an eternity later I was in my car headed for Doctor Carlson. After he examined me he declared that I would have to stay on total bed rest from now until the babies' birth. My cervix was thinning and we needed to buy as much time as possible. I was so grateful I wasn't in labor. My job seemed of little importance now. Attending the meeting certainly hadn't been worth the risk and could have undone everything we had worked years to accomplish.

At home, Danny adapted to my bedrest orders like a pro. He waited on me continually bringing me the newspaper, mail, drinks, and food, and he kept me company. My constant couch and bed companions during the day were our pets, Boom-boom and Special. There was nothing more enjoyable for them than napping with their humans. Much of my quiet time was spent in prayer for the health and safe birth of the babies.

A source of irritation during this time were television reports or newspaper items in which some "authority" expounded on their opinion of our choice. One renowned ethnologist claimed what we were doing was,

We made the most of bedrest with a bedtime story for Lucas, Clay and Cole.

"Very, very, very bad for the children..." Christa and I really flipped about this. Christa exclaimed, "He doesn't even know us. How can he make a blanket statement like that for the world to hear without meeting us!" Thankfully another ethics expert who is a regular on *Good Morning America* rebutted the statement saying he felt it was the most perfect solution to this problem. A mother would never try to withhold the baby from her daughter. A daughter would never renege on taking the child. None of the muddy waters from previous surrogate cases were likely to be issues when a family makes a decision like this together.

Many news programs and "expert" interviews included speculation about how I would feel about these babies once they were born. Even close friends expressed their concern that I would be too attached to let them go or that I would love them more than my other grandchildren. I knew that I was just sitting on the nest for Christa. A human incubator. As for loving them more than my other grandchildren, it wasn't possible.

Danny voiced his analysis of the issue during an interview with an Australian television show. "Fathers don't carry their children to term," he said. "Are you implying they cannot possibly love their children as much as the mother who carries them?"

Carrying a child and giving birth aren't the main determininants in the parent-child bond. Parental commitment, nurturing, and caring for the emotional, spiritual and physical needs of a child are far more important. Sadly, there are mothers and fathers who are unable to make that commitment to their children. But these babies were blessed with two fine parents who were waiting to take on this responsibility as soon as they were born.

While I was on bedrest, Christa and Kevin were frequent visitors. Christa used a stethoscope to listened to her babies in the womb and we went to my checkups together so we could share this experience as a family. That fall, Christa and Kevin were also in the process of moving to Rapid City. Kevin had been an employee with Nash Finch since he was a teenager. In Sioux City, he held the position of assistant manager in a large grocery store. It was unusual for someone to be transferred from one district to another and his district did not include Rapid City, but we were thrilled when he was promoted to manager and assigned to a new store in Rapid City. With Curtis and Gina already in Rapid City, it would bring the family closer together.

While Kevin was finishing his work in Iowa, Christa was looking for a house in Rapid City. I would have loved to have helped her search, but my condition meant she was on her own.

A mere six days after they were settled into their home in Rapid City, I was scheduled for another doctor's appointment. Christa flew to Aberdeen for the checkup on October 11 because Kevin could not come until the following day. He had a store meeting he had to attend and planned to drive to Aberdeen the next day and spend the weekend. The two would then drive back to Rapid City together. We also had a reporter and photographer from *Life Choices,* a Ohio health magazine, scheduled to visit us on the same day as the appointment.

During the *Life Choices* interview, I told the reporter, "I don't think I will be carrying these babies until my due date in November."

He asked, "Why?"

I laughingly told him, "My body is saying soon, this weekend probably."

The pictures taken of Danny and me that day show a happy and loving couple, one very pregnant person and one looking very proud.

Our appointment went so well that Doctor Carlson thought we should go out for lunch. It was my first public outing in a month and the patrons at the restaurant were encouraging and supportive.

Earlier in the pregnancy, when the media stories began, Danny was in a small town selling Keebler products. He was approached by a man in a local restaurant who said, "You're from Aberdeen. Do you know the woman who is going to give birth to her grandchildren?"

"That's my wife," Dan answered.

"You're kidding. No way!" the man replied.

It took a little convincing, but soon everyone in the restaurant had to shake Danny's hand. That's South Dakota.

Most South Dakotans are friendly and informal without being forward or presumptuous. It felt so good to see friends and neighbors at lunch that day, and it was certainly a nice break from my bedrest routine.

Christa called Kevin to report the latest news about the twins.

"Mom's intuition is telling her that the birth may take place this weekend," she relayed.

Christa was concerned about Kevin having to drive to Aberdeen late at night, especially after a long work day. The two decided he would leave early the next morning. That was a mistake.

That evening, with a Minnesota Twins baseball game playing in the background, Christa and I started sorting baby clothes. These were clothes that had been hers, Curtis' and Chad's when they were babies. I had saved them in a cedar chest. As we looked at an outfit that had been Chad's, Christa mentioned that she and Kevin were thinking of using Chad's name for their son.

"Would it bother you?" she asked.

"Not at all," I replied.

"We would be so proud," her dad interjected.

At that moment I felt a twinge and a release of moisture. I waddled toward the bathroom stating, "I think my water just broke."

"Oh, you get so excited over every little twinge," Danny teased.

I could hear the two of them laughing about how I exaggerated everything.

"Somebody get me a towel... and somebody better call Kevin," I called back. You should have seen those two. It was right out of an "I Love Lucy" sketch. They both moved fast, ran into one another and accomplished nothing. I laughed at them as I got my own towel, took my overnight case to the door and gathered the cameras.

Christa made it to the phone and called Doctor Carlson at home to tell him what was happening. Her next call was to Kevin. She could not reach him and I could tell she was getting stressed. This was before cell phones were commonplace, so the next best thing to do was to call Curtis

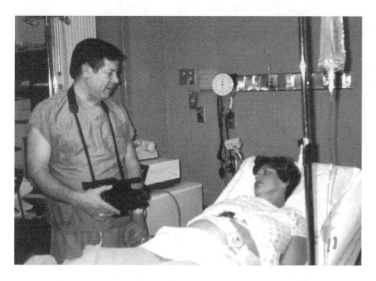

Ready to go. Arlette and Danny wait in the labor room while Christa tries to reach Kevin on the phone.

phones were commonplace, so the next best thing to do was to call Curtis and Gina. They could try to find Kevin while we headed to the hospital.

When we arrived at Saint Luke's Hospital we were greeted by security people who escorted us to the labor room. I slipped into a gown and a nurse strapped a contraction monitor around my belly. As soon as I was settled, the first labor pain washed over me. The intensity indicator went to the very peak of the monitor.

Christa repeatedly dialed home to Rapid City. Hopes were fast fading that both parents would be able to attend the birth. I felt like all it would take was one good push and it would be over. Fortunately, it didn't take Doctor Carlson long to arrive.

"I think we better do a Caesarean," he concluded after making his examination.

I was dismayed at first. My other childbirth experiences were vaginal, plus I wanted to be awake.

"You'll still remain conscious for the birth," he assured me. "You just won't have much sensation."

"But I think with a little time and one good push this will be over," I told him. I could see he wasn't convinced, so I asked, "Okay, if this were your wife and children, what would you recommend?"

"The problem is that the smaller baby is definitely in breech position. He or she will come out feet first and that is not a good thing," he explained. I agreed that we should do whatever would be safest for the babies, so the birth would be by C-section.

Christa finally reached Kevin at home. Well in advance, they had gotten the names of several local pilots who could fly him to Aberdeen in case of an emergency. He started calling them, but was soon disappointed to find all the pilots were either out of the region, or had flown their quota of miles that day.

Doctor Carlson said he would wait as long as he safely could before starting the surgery. The obstetric team were being called and we would wait until they were all assembled. One of them was Christa's pediatrician and the doctor who first discovered her syndrome, Dr. Heinemann. She would attend to the twins.

Curtis had been busy readying his van and family for the six-hour drive to Aberdeen. Once on the road, Curtis, Gina and Kevin spent anxious hours driving with no information about the status of the delivery. Blissfully, the three boys slept the trip and night away.

It was after midnight on October 12, when I was wheeled into surgery. The room continued to fill with people. Danny stood with his video camera at my feet. Christa was near my left. Two anesthesiologists were on my right. The rest of the room seemed filled to capacity with medical personnel. Fortunately, there was room for my focal point, Doctor Carlson, and for Doctor Heinemann.

A spinal nerve block was administered, but after waiting the allotted time I could still feel everything. I overheard the anesthetist talking about an epidural and I asked if it was safe to do both. Someone said something about being able to walk after both treatments. Doctor Carlson quickly interjected, "She will be fine."

I felt better because I had complete trust in him. The labor pains continued and I was holding back for the sake of the little ones. It took as much energy not to push as it did to endure the labor.

Finally, the feeling from my waist down was gone. It seemed like just seconds later when I felt a slight tugging sensation. Doctor Carlson held up a tiny bundle and exclaimed, "It's a boy!"

Christa and I both started crying.

A couple minutes later I heard Danny say with an emotion-filled voice, "It's a girl!"

Christa was crying hard by now and she leaned toward me and said, "I love you, Mom."

"I love you, too. Now go to your babies."

My eyes followed her as she went to their incubators and pulled her mask back to kiss their tiny feet. It was a moment I will never forget.

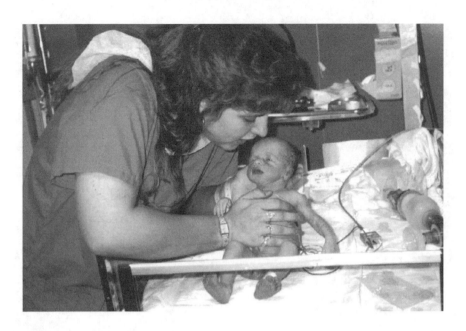

*Christa is shown here with her new infant
son about five minutes after his birth.*

Then the room erupted with cheering and clapping. It seemed that everyone realized simultaneously that something had just taken place that had never before happened in the United States. As far as C-section births go, this one had been unremarkable – except that here, in a midwestern town in South Dakota, a woman had given birth to her own grandchildren. We were all pioneers.

The babies were beautiful. I could see that Christa's baby girl was much smaller than her brother. But she seemed more alert. She was wide-eyed and looking around. The boy seemed to be in some distress and Doctor Heinemann quickly administered oxygen to him as she reassured Christa that he would be fine.

The noise subsided and the room cleared almost as quickly as it had filled. Most of the team followed the babies up to the maternity ward where a special unit was waiting for them. I would join them shortly. For now I was content in the recovery room, drifting in and out of sleep, covered in a warmed blanket. My part was over and my responsibility lifted. The babies were in the hands of specialists who would take good care of them. I was a relieved and tired grandmother, thankful to God for the birth of her two newest grandchildren.

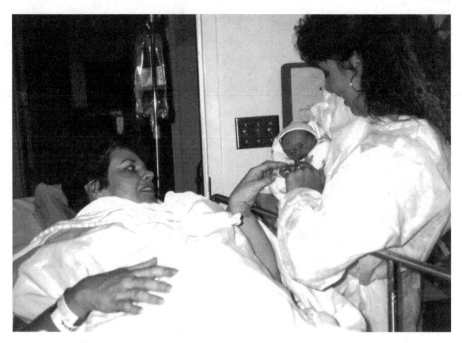

Becoming a grandparent is a magical experience.
Here, I greet Chelsea for the first time.

Sometime later, I was wheeled to the room that Christa and I would share. It was nearly three in the morning. Waiting patiently in the hall outside my room were my own dear mother and my sister Marlis. Mom said, "I wanted to see how MY daughter was doing."

I knew this was not an easy wait for my mother. She had endured three separate open heart surgeries and one angioplasty. But her failing heart did not obstruct her loving heart. There was no other place on earth she would rather have been. Of course, she was also anticipating seeing her newest great-grandchildren. All the months of worrying about me and fretting about our unusual situation were finally over. She looked lovingly at the two babies in the isolettes and knew it had all been worthwhile.

About an hour later Christa saw Kevin coming down the hall. The two of them went immediately to the nursery so they could spend some private time together with their children. I heard familiar voices in the hall and was quickly surrounded by Curtis, Gina and their three boys. Lucas, Clay and Cole all came for hugs and kisses. Then they wanted to see the babies. A short time later, Kevin and Christa came into the room and sat on Christa's bed.

"Kevin and I have already decided on names for the babies," Christa said. "They are going to be Chad Daniel and Chelsea Arlette."

I was speechless. I had no idea they were even thinking along those lines, but I was thrilled and I still consider it an honor and loving tribute each time I hear those names.

Our room started to fill with flowers and with visitors. Baskets and vases with gorgeous bouquets started arriving. Many were from producers and television personalities. Sally Jesse Raphel sent everything in red. Maury Povich and Connie Chung sent flowers in an antique-looking vase. The producer with whom we decided to work on a movie version of our story sent a basket as large as a card table. The card read, "To the best producers of all."

Our visitors were limited to family, but our family is large including Dan's parents, brother and sister and their families; my mom plus my six sisters and brothers. Our attorney friend, Rory King was also there to handle all the publicity calls and organize a press conference. A separate phone line had been added at the hospital just to direct all the media calls to Rory's office. This took the pressure off the hospital. They had their hands full controlling and intercepting all the media people who started descending like raindrops from the sky.

"Here we go again," I thought. But I didn't begrudge people wanting to share in our joy.

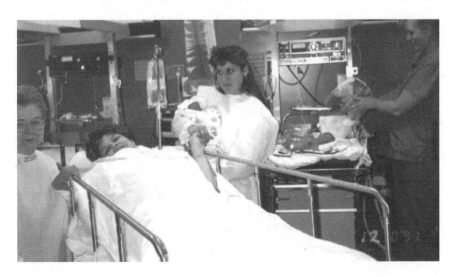

Shortly after their birth, the twins are seen here with Mom Christa, Grandmother Arlette and Great-Grandmother Mary Friesz Rafferty.

Chapter 22

Life After Birth

The birth of the twins brought another flurry of media attention. They descended on our families from across the country, and once again we were inundated with calls, reporters and photographers.

The hospital and our attorney, Rory King, scheduled a press conference thinking this would help stifle the flood of people trying to see us. At the last minute it was decided the babies could be present for this event. The room was filled with photographers, reporters and television cameras as well as medical personnel and my mother and sisters.

The event went wonderfully with our son-in-law summing it up. "It's been a fairy tale from beginning to end." We all agreed.

After the press conference we thought the media interest would subside. We were wrong.

Calls continued from media the world over. Everyone seemed interested in and excited about the birth of a boy and girl who had been carried to term by their grandmother. Letters began pouring in from nearly every country in the world. We were overwhelmed by the thoughtfulness, support and kind words people expressed. Surprisingly, nearly half the letters we received were written by men.

It was also amazing that the post office was able to route letters with partial or cryptic addresses. One came addressed to "Twentieth Century Pioneer." Many letters were simply addressed to "Grandmother, Aberdeen, SD." There were beautiful, sensitive letters that touched our hearts. Christa and I tried to answer every piece of mail. We looked forward to the daily deliveries and reading through the mounds of letters each day.

Only two letters had negative content. One was just plain freaky. It contained mostly garbled and nonsensical blather about black leather. It was actually frightening and I should have contacted the New York police because the writer was obviously one strange individual. The other came from a lady in South Dakota who thought we had done "a very bad thing." The letter upset me and I should have dismissed it. I felt that if she could just meet us, and I could talk to her, she would feel differently.

I was discharged from the hospital amidst a flutter of cameras and well-wishers. Chad and Chelsea needed to stay a few days longer. Chad, the larger of the twins and the one who was eager to get things rolling, was still having respiratory problems. It wasn't anything severe, but he needed to stay in an incubator to be monitored. Chelsea, who weighed only four pounds at birth, was gaining weight and strength steadily. Christa and Kevin stayed at the hospital with the twins so they could feed and hold them whenever possible.

Because of our family experience with Sudden Infant Death Syndrome, I wanted the twins to have infant monitors when they left the hospital. It eased my mind greatly when I learned these had been ordered.

The day finally arrived when the twins were allowed to go home. It was difficult to find the words to express our gratitude to Doctors Carlson and Heinemann, the wonderful staff and the Presentation Sisters at St. Luke's, Rory King, and all of our supporters and family. Cheers went up

At the press conference after the twins' birth, Kevin summed up the situation saying, "It's been a fairy tale from beginning to end."

as our little group left the hospital. Christa and Kevin made a brief stop at our home to change diapers. We gave them goodbye hugs and then the Uchytils were off to Rapid City.

Were there tears? Did I experience a wrenching loss?

Not at all.

After Kevin, Christa and the twins left, Danny and I sat down together in our home and shared a quiet moment. He put his arm around me and I rested my head on his shoulder.

"How do you feel?" he asked.

"I'm content and relieved," I said. "My part is over, now. The rest is up to Christa and Kevin."

I felt enveloped by a warm sense of fulfillment and happiness. I love the twins dearly, but from the moment I saw their first ultrasound I knew that I loved them as my grandchildren, just like I loved Lucas, Clay and Cole.

Christa and Kevin were going to have their hands full. Christa would be a new mom with two babies and she would get very little sleep. I wished we lived closer so I could have helped her. When she reported that the twins alternated their waking times, I really wished I could be there. As soon as Christa got Chad to sleep, Chelsea would awaken.

The twins (about age 2) with Mom and Dad at our Aberdeen home.

Fortunately, Christa's joy overrode her exhaustion and carried her through the long days and nights of mixing formula, changing diapers and answering monitor alarms.

When Christa and Kevin moved to Rapid City, they wisely opted for an unlisted telephone number. That meant they were spared the constant interruption they would no doubt have otherwise endured. One positive aspect of all the publicity was that our story reached many other victims of Mayer-Rokitansky-Kuster-Hauser Syndrome. I received a number of calls from young women who had been diagnosed with the syndrome and I got Christa's permission before giving out her phone number. Christa always took the time to talk with anyone needing help coping with this devastating condition. Parents of those afflicted also wrote and called us. Some wanted information. Others wanted to connect with someone they knew could understand. One elderly woman wrote to us with a heartbreaking story of surgery and atrocities that had been heaped on her when she was young. Christa and I corresponded with her as well as many young girls and their mothers. Christa was a real inspiration to those worrying about a normal married life.

For us, another positive aspect of the media attention was tangible evidence of the goodness of people from all cultures and walks of life. Most people, no matter where they live or what their beliefs, love and want the best for their children. With all the sadness, abuse and destruction in the world, people thought it was refreshing to find a headline about family love with no underlying motive. We were gratified to learn that our story had touched the hearts of many. In return, many people touched our hearts.

After the twins' birth, we received a steady stream of requests from national talk shows. Most of these shows were looking for sensational programming rather than serving as a forum to educate or inspire. We turned them down over and over. We did agree to appear on several news programs, and even travelled to Spain to be on television there. We turned down trips to England and Germany, much to Dan's disappointment. I've never been keen on air travel and our trip to Spain involved a flight from Madrid to Valencia where the engines quit for a short period of time. That and some other unfortunate flying experiences left me with a greater fear of flying than I had in the beginning.

I preferred to participate in shows that could be taped at our home. When we did fly, it took major effort on my part because of the anxiety I felt. I also made it clear that I would not fly into a city for a show one day and fly home the next. I needed time to regroup between flights.

Many television schedulers pitch how much fun you will have on their programs. They make it sound like a free vacation. Not so. It is always work, it always costs money, and it is not always that much fun.

One exception was our trip to New York to appear on a new show with Maury Povich. His producers agreed to fly our entire family to New York City for the appearance. My sister, Darlene, and her husband also flew to New York so they could watch from the audience. The show went well and we had an unforgettable time in New York. Later Maury Provich and his wife Connie Chung sent the twins matching cribs for a gift.

Amid all of this excitement I went back to work. It was good to be back in school with friends, students and a routine. Our television trips were taken on school breaks and vacations so I didn't miss any actual school days. I turned down many requests because they conflicted with my work schedule. A lot of the schedulers couldn't understand my work ethic and I got used to telling them "no thanks" when they exclaimed, "But this is the chance of a lifetime!" *Oprah* was the one show on which we would have loved to appear. Christa and I, like most everyone, admire Oprah, but we couldn't abandon our responsibilities and the show does no taping in the summer.

Slowly and gradually life returned to normal. We continue to receive requests for follow-up stories from time to time and our story has been featured in several books about life, babies, surrogacy, and SIDS. We've even been mentioned in college textbooks. But, Christa and Kevin have managed to shield Chad and Chelsea from a lot of the attention. I think they have enjoyed a normal childhood.

When the twins were in the first grade, *People Magazine* wanted photos and an update. After many hours of being photographed, we went our for a family dinner. Chelsea was in one car with me, while Dan rode with Christa and Chad.

Chelsea turned to me and asked, "Why do people want to take our pictures, Grandma?"

"Well Chelsea, why do you think that is?" I asked.

"I think it's because Chad and I are twins, and you're a librarian."

I smiled and answered, "I think you're right."

We are often asked if Chad and Chelsea know about the unique and special way they came into this world. Yes, they know that I carried them for their mom because she didn't have a uterus. They also know they are from their parents, Christa and Kevin, and that I just sat on the nest.

Hanging on the wall outside their bedrooms is a picture of me the day before they were born. There are many others taken with their parents in the days after their birth. Our home also has framed pictures of magazine covers and articles that featured us. Chad and Chelsea do not even notice them. It is normal to them and for our other grandchildren.

We make no big deal out of it because it is no big deal to us. In fact, it is something we can forget about. I do not look at the twins and think, "I gave birth to them." Unless I am consciously reminded it doesn't even enter my mind. I don't think Christa thinks about it either because once when we were talking about her syndrome, Christa said "Well, I'd just do for her like you did for me." Then, we realized what she had said and we both burst out laughing. It really made us think about how we DON'T think about it.

Another time out of the blue Chelsea said, "Grandma, when I grow up are you going to have babies for me?"

"If you need me to I will, Chelsea," I answered. "But you will probably be able to carry your own babies." I'm trying to stay healthy, just in case!

Chapter 23

Labor of Love: The Movie

Before the birth of the twins, we developed a rapport with movie producer Phil Leviton. He flew to Aberdeen to meet us and instead of trying to impress us with a lot of name-dropping and Hollywood jargon, he showed us examples of projects for which he and his partner Alfred Kelman had responsiblity. Their company was called KLM Productions and they ultimately made us an offer to produce a movie version of our story. Even though it was substantially less than some of the other offers, we liked that KLM promised to give us complete story approval rights. Other production companies wanted full story rights meaning they could fictionalize and sensationalize the story at their discretion. We wanted something that truly reflected our family and that was representative of our values. In particular, we wanted something of which we could be proud.

We signed an agreement with KLM and this brought more people to shadow us at home and work. Producers and writers came to work with me. They traveled with us to Lemmon when we visited family. They shared our meals with us and interviewed friends and family. The screen writer, Susan Baskin, was a wonderful person. She was sensitive and interested in portraying us accurately. It became natural to share family events and details of our life with her. Tears were shed as we told her about Chad's death; laughter when we talked about me being a Bobby Vee groupie. She even tied that to the movie by using the Bobby Vee hit *"Take Good Care of My Baby"* as the opening song.

Emmy-award-winning actress Ann Jillian was signed to play me. I had always admired her and coincidentally we were featured on opposite pages in a magazine I had purchased shortly before. There was a picture of me and a photo and story about Ann Jillian who was also about to give birth to her firth child at the age of forty-two. Her mannerisms were so much like mine. She likes to dress in jeans and sweatshirts like I do. Her Catholic faith is an important part of her life as is mine and we both gave birth at the age of 42.

Tracey Gold was chosen to play the part of Christa. The script had the dialogue right but Tracey was challenged to capture Christa's personality. The actor that played Dan was right on the money and Canadian-born Donal Logue, chosen to play Kevin, was a dead ringer in looks and personality. It was uncanny!

The movie was filmed in Wilmington, South Carolina, the Hollywood of the East Coast. Each day a Federal Express truck would deliver a script to our home in Aberdeen where we would edit or supplement it. Then we would send the script back. Toward the end of the filming our entire family was invited to the set. They had done an amazing job of duplicating Aberdeen with signs on buildings indicating Simmons Junior High and St. Luke's Hospital. All the cars on the set had South Dakota license plates. It was surreal. As I stepped out of our car, Ann Jillian

Along with my sister Darlene, Christa and Gina, I got to meet my favorite singer – Bobby Vee. His hit "Take Good Care of My Baby" was used for the opening of "Labor of Love."

139

Christa and actress Tracey Gold, who portrayed her in the made for television movie of our story

came out of her trailer. We ran to one another like old friends and hugged. As we walked around the movie set we were surprised to discover our names on the trailers belonging to the stars who were playing us.

Our days were spent watching the filming and eating the great food that was continually refurbished for those involved in the film. We were introduced to producers, directors, actors, and makeup artists. As we took pictures of Ann Jillian, she was taking pictures of us. A house had been rented to portray our home in Aberdeen. We learned that the house was what is called a "hot set." Filming had already taken place there and there would be additional scenes to be shot. Nothing could be touched or moved. They had even replicated our family pictures on the walls but the faces in the photos were the stars of the film! Filming also took place in a real grocery store, a real school and a fake hospital.

The grandboys were especially well-behaved. Of course the twins were too young to understand what was going on, but were wide-eyed at all the activity. My daughter-in-law Gina even got a walk-on part, and so did my sister Darlene. As a surprise to me when we went to watch the filming I was offered a speaking part – the role of my library assistant Pam. I nearly turned it down because we had planned to take the grandkids to the beach and I did not want to disappoint them. Dan wouldn't let me refuse feeling I would really enjoy the experience and he was right. They all made me feel good by calling me "One-take Arlette."

There were only a couple of inaccuracies that we missed in the script. The major error was at the end of the movie. It shows me saying to

140

Christa, "You are the love of my life." This hurt me when I saw it because Dan is the love of my life. Christa and Curtis are my children and I love them with my whole heart. I would lay down my life for them, but Danny is my soul mate, my love, my life. However, the end result, *"Labor of Love: The Arlette Schweitzer Story,"* was a solid, honest story of love, family and faith. We were proud when it first aired in 1993.

Dan and I are very proud of our grandsons Lucas, Clay and Cole. As young adults, they have grown into fine young men who continue to include us in our life.

Chapter 24

The Best Is Yet to Come

The twins are nearly teenagers – and miraculously I am still 42. I ascribe this to my philosophy that years are not as much a measure of age as is attitude. If I start thinking I'm old, I will feel too old to make changes in my life, or go on that hike, or act silly with my sister. It's ironic for someone who looks back at her childhood and thinks she was "born old."

In October 2002, twin girls were born in Sturgis, South Dakota. The birth made headlines because like me, their grandmother carried the twins for her daughter. Sharon Dunn contacted me shortly after Chad and Chelsea's birth. She had read about us and asked if Christa would talk to her daughter Trisha. They had found out that 14-year-old Trisha was born without her uterus. I called Christa who willingly took time from her new babies to visit Trisha. Trisha was encouraged that this devastating syndrome didn't dash any future hopes she might have for having children of her own. Christa's visit made a difference in young Trisha's life and we are grateful for that. Many people probably wonder why families affected by this syndrome don't simply adopt, but that alternative can have drawbacks and even heartbreak of its own.

Over the years we maintained contact with the Dunns. In early 2002, Sharon called to tell me that after a heartbreaking adoption failure they were going to try to repeat what we had done. I gave Sharon as much advice and encouragement as I could and told her we would pray for them. In August, Sharon called to tell me they were expecting twins. Their birth in 2003 rekindled interest in our story.

We agreed to go on *The John Walsh Show* when he did a program

142

John Walsh contacted us for his program dedicated to mothers who do extraordinary things for their children.

devoted to "Mothers who have done extraordinary things for their children." Chad and Chelsea were excited about a trip to New York, and their eyes nearly popped when a stretch limousine picked us up at the airport. Chad said, "I could get used to this!"

Meeting John Walsh was fantastic for all of us. He is as nice as he seems on television. It was a new experience for Chad and Chelsea and they enjoyed all the action "behind the scenes" at the program. It was Chelsea's turn to say "I could get used to this" when professionals applied our makeup before the show.

The show was great fun but I think both twins were happy when we headed back to South Dakota and home. The limos are gone, New York is far away and the thrill of being part of a movie featuring our lives is in the past.

People sometimes say to me, "That must have been the best time of your life." It was an experience of a lifetime, and one that I am happy to have had, but there are many other highlights. Learning to talk to and trust God with my heart. When my children were born. Welcoming a daughter and son-in-law we love into our family. Holding each of my grandchildren in my arms. Family time together. But the best time of my life is every moment I spend with Danny.

And the best is yet to come.

Kevin, Christa, Chelsea and Chad.

Chapter 25

My Beliefs

"Never doubt that a small group of people can change the world. It is the only thing that ever has."
–Margaret Mead

The Schweitzers are a typical middle class family, with middle class values. What is important to Dan and me is important to most families. Our family, our faith, our friends, our home, our pets, our country, our work and our love for each other.

Those of us who care about these things must make a statement. Our world is changing and not all the advances are for the good of humanity. We need to speak out about the things that are corroding our world and the future of our children.

We need harsher penalties for those that buy and sell pornography and drugs. It should be "one strike and you're out" for pedophiles. We should promote respect for people, property, animals, and our environment. Teach tolerance for those that look, act and think differently than ourselves. Model good manners and teach consideration for all human life.

How can we change the world? Here is a summary of the beliefs by which I live, and by which Dan and I have tried to raise our family.

1. Pray to worship and grow in your relationship with God.
2. Don't use foul language or take out anger on others
3. Take time to go to church and to commune with others.
4. Respect the elderly, especially our parents.
5. Don't kill.
6. Take your wedding vows seriously.
7. Stealing, is stealing, is stealing.

8. Tell the truth.

9. Be grateful for what you have.

10. The grass is not always greener on the other side.

And finally, (Matthew 7:12) treat others as you would have them treat you.

Doesn't this all sound familiar? Of course, God said it first, and more eloquently. God bless each of you who took time to read my story.

-Arlette Rafferty Schweitzer (still age 42)

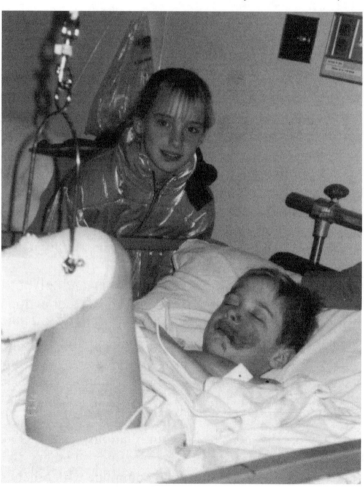

Chelsea visits Chad in the hospital following his injury as the result of being struck by a car.

Epilogue

Our lives continue to be filled with happiness, heartache and triumph. Danny was in a terrible car accident that required two stomach surgeries. A car hit Chad when he was a third grader and threw him 26 feet. His femur was shattered along the growth plate. While I was writing this in 2003, he was at the Mayo Clinic undergoing yet another surgery that was a direct result of that trauma. In the summer of 2003, Danny was diagnosed with stage four dysplasia of the colon. He underwent a total removal of his colon, resulting in an ileostomy surgery at the Mayo Clinic. Yet, each bump in the road makes us stronger and draws us even closer.

Our family prays together, suffers together and laughs together. When one of us is hurting, we all are hurting. And right now we are hurting for Chad.

Chad, a natural athlete, started limping and hurting in June 2003. Christa took him back to the surgeon who performed the initial surgery following his accident. Following a bone scan, it was determined he needed to build up the muscle in the leg. So, he went to physical therapy three times a week and also played hockey. He exercised and played in pain.

After six months without improvement, another surgeon diagnosed a serious slippage of the growth plate known as a Slipped Capital Femoral Epiphysis (SCFE). Chad should have received specialized treatment for this condition back in June. Too late, we learned that exercise was the worst possible course for SCFE.

Upon hearing the diagnosis, I immediately wanted to call Doctor William Phipps, the doctor responsible for Chad and Chelsea being here in the first place. He now lives in New York, and I was able to reach him at his home. His calm voice was reassuring, and his advice was sound. He remains our hero!

Naturally, Christa and Kevin are upset about this latest setback for Chad. Chelsea is especially sad for her "twin" and her best friend, and his older cousins, Lucas, Clay and Cole, are praying for him.

In spite of these setbacks, we are grateful for the many blessings God has bestowed upon us. They are tangible evidence of the hand of God at work. As a final note, I should mention that because women with Mayer-Rokitansky-Kuster-Hauser Syndrome previously had no offspring, there were no available data about whether the abnormality was an inherited trait. The disorder only affects women and with Chelsea's birth there was finally a "next generation" to study. Fortunately, Chelsea has no abnormalities and I won't have to make good on my promise to carry children for her. How then, do I feel about the miracle of the twins? Do I feel a special blessing was bestowed on us? Yes, I do. I do not know why, and I do not feel worthy. I just know He allowed us this special blessing in one of His many demonstrations of love.

We are blessed that we are together on our many-seated bicycle. We keep pedaling, knowing the Lord is steering from the front seat.

In 1996, I was inducted into the South Dakota Hall of Fame. Lucas, Clay and Cole were there to share the excitement.

The first I heard of **Mayer-Rokitansky-Kuster-Hauser** Syndrome was the day Doctor Heinemann told Christa and me about her condition. Subsequently, we learned more about the varying degrees of involvement and came to appreciate how truly fortunate Christa is.

Some of what we learned was directly related to the publicity we were getting. People from all walks of life, and from all over the world, contacted us to share their personal experiences. Mothers, fathers and those afflicted themselves wanted to glean what they could from us. It brought this syndrome to the surface and for the first time people were openly talking about it. The medical world was especially interested because no one with this syndrome had ever before had children.

MRKH affects only females and we know that about one in every four-to-five thousand women has the syndrome. Those born with Mayer-Rokintansky-Kuster-Hauser Syndrome have one feature in common. They do not menstruate because they do not have a uterus. Thus, the syndrome is usually not discovered until late adolescence when the lack of menstruation becomes a concern. They may or may not have any of the other features of the disorder which include: short or non-existent vagina, one kidney or horseshoe shaped kidneys, and skeletal malformations.

I have read that ovarian function is preserved in women with this syndrome, but we were told this is not always the case.

The cause of MRKH syndrome is unknown and no known gene has been linked to it. While medical treatment can repair and deal with many of the physical aspects of this syndrome, the psychological issues also need to be addressed.

Christa has visited with many young women and reassured them that life can be normal. I personally feel those who have this condition need to seek out others to share their heartbreak and their successes. We also have the internet to help women connect about this devastating condition.

Good luck to all those that have MRKH syndrome and know that God has something special in store for you too.

—Arlette

Home in One Piece

"An inspirational story of hope and endurance."
-Joan Lunden

In 1992, young **John Thompson** lost both arms in a tragic accident. Thanks to his dog Tuffy, Thompson survived to share this powerful story of courage including the untold story of how being catapulted into the media spotlight changed his life and impacted his family. John and writer Paula Crain Grosinger have used this book to raise over $6,000.00 for local charities.

Visit www.johnsbook.net   ISBN 0-9720054-0-4
168 pages of text plus additional photo pages.

Retail $16.95
Dogs are heroes, too!

Lily in the Rain
Poetry by Donald Hoffman
Retail price $6.95

Donald Hoffman taught at the American College and Roberts College in Istanbul, Turkey where he lived for 26 years. His stirring work reflects Middle East and Western philosophies. A distinguished musicologist, Mr. Hoffman was also a long-time announcer with North Dakota Public Radio.

ISBN 0-9724340-0-3

Children Heard
"I love you More than Chocolate"
offers practical advice for parents and grandparents to help children heal when mom and dad divorce. The book includes artwork by children that is expressive of their feelings about divorce and growing up. Bismarck author Marcia Tabram Philips also offers step-by-step instructions for building positive memories to last a lifetime.

Retail price $19.95

To order call **877-566-2665** toll-free, or mail payment to:

Crain Grosinger Publishing, P.O. Box 55, Mandan, ND 58554
Check, Money Order, VISA, Mastercard accepted.

Ask about school and book club discounts.
Sales taxes and US shipping are included.